THE ACTIVITY
ILLUSION

THE ACTIVITY
ILLUSION

WHY WE LIVE TO WORK IN THE 21ST CENTURY
– AND HOW TO WORK TO LIVE INSTEAD

IAN PRICE

Matador
5 Weir Road
Kibworth Beauchamp
Leicester LE8 0LQ, UK
Tel: (+44) 116 279 2299
Fax: (+44) 116 279 2277
Email: books@troubador.co.uk
Web: www.troubador.co.uk/matador

ISBN 978 1848769 496

British Library Cataloguing in Publication Data.
A catalogue record for this book is available from the British Library.

Typeset in 12pt Bembo by Troubador Publishing Ltd, Leicester, UK
Printed and bound in Great Britain by TJI Digital, Padstow, Cornwall

Matador is an imprint of Troubador Publishing Ltd

For Iyabo

ACKNOWLEDGEMENTS

The author would like to thank the following people for their help, guidance and support in writing this book: My literary agent Diane Banks; Nathan Zeldes; Professor Cary Cooper; Philip Sheldrake; Carl French; Mike Trenouth; David Sales; Angus Porter; Ivor Kellock; Polly Courtney and Paul Morland.

CONTENTS

Introduction:
"A four day week and then three days' fun"   1

Chapter 1:
Entering the Karoshi Zone   9

Chapter 2:
"Email is Ruining My Life" (Part One)   25

Chapter 3:
"Email is Ruining My Life" (Part Two): "Addiction is a Choice"   38

Chapter 4:
Status Indicators –
The Death of Hierarchy and the Birth of Hyperactivity   55

Chapter 5:
"Lunch is for Wimps": The Rise of Aggression   61

Chapter 6:
Taming the Technology Beast   70

Chapter 7:
Focus   98

Chapter 8:
Leadership: "The Fish Rots from the Head"   116

Chapter 9:
People   128

Chapter 10:
Freedom from Hyperactivity: The Virtuous Circle   165

Endnote   193

Appendix: Dan Loeb Email   197

References   203

Index   207

INTRODUCTION

"A four-day week, and then three days' fun."

It is the summer of 1953. Winston Churchill, Britain's Prime Minister, is in bed at Chequers recovering from a stroke and being examined by his doctor, Lord Moran. Churchill, who thought deeply about the technological advances brought about by science, shared his vision of an end to the Cold War. "If it came off," he said to Moran, "and there was disarmament, production might be doubled and we might be able to give the working man what he has never had – leisure. A four-day week, and then three days' fun."[i]

This aspiration of giving the worker a three-day weekend may seem a fantasy today but was not so far-fetched at the time. Some fifty years earlier, workers in manufacturing industries had only recently ceased the practice of working a full day on Saturday. The change was a result of the establishment of Trade Unions pushing back against eighteen-hour shifts and the technological innovations that drove improvements in productivity. It was the Edwardian practice of allowing workers Saturday afternoons off work that led to the boom in professional football clubs with legions of paying fans. So, in the 1950s – an age of continuing scientific advancement - it did not seem unrealistic to pursue a vision of increased leisure.

Fast-forward another fifty years from Churchill's premiership and against a backdrop of accelerating and dizzying technological advancement, here is a pen–portrait of his twenty–first century successor written by Iain Martin in *The Daily Telegraph*. Describing the weekend preparation for Gordon Brown's visit to the US, Martin writes:

"By Sunday Team Brown will be suffering from severe sleep deprivation, taking phone calls and emails from the PM around the clock. Most likely, the advisers will have an agreed text signed off only as they board the plane for Washington. And only then will Brown decide that he does not like the prepared speech. At that point he will, I confidently predict, start bashing out a new one on a laptop. Head down, his hands a blur, as they have been thousands of times down the years, this is how Brown always works."[ii]

While this is an imagined scene rather than a documentary description, it is an elegant summary of the leadership style that is evident in both the political and corporate classes of the twenty-first century – rich in technology but poor in effectiveness. The frenetic blur of activity straddling a weekend, the meddling in detail, the frenzy of digital communication all raise questions about the leader's sense of perspective and the ability to delegate. The same behaviours are just as evident in the corporate world. "My family are used to not seeing me during the week," says one CEO interviewed in *The Secrets of CEOs* by Steve Tappin and Andrew Cave. "They see me at weekends but not all the time or every weekend." "I can't remember my boys growing up," says another.[iii] As this book will show, it is not just the CEOs of organisations that are affected, since the impact of this way of working trickles down the hierarchy. In many ways, however, the CEOs are far better equipped to cope than more junior employees.

So how is it that, after decades of technological and economic advancement we have not only failed to deliver Churchill's vision of a leisure society but, for many of us, we have gone backwards with even the two-day weekend being eroded by work?

This book examines why we work the way we do and asks the question whether or not our heightened levels of activity make us more productive and effective in our jobs or happier in our lives. Churchill's primary concern was for the working man in an era when it was not unheard of for a paternalistic board of company directors to sleep off a big lunch after a board meeting while a retainer wheeled round the drinks trolley. Another Prime Minister of the era, Macmillan, said in a radio interview that one of the aspects of being Prime Minister that he most liked was that he found so much time to read Victorian fiction. Today, in the post-industrial age, there is evidence that the imbalance has become reversed, with managers and leaders now working harder than anyone else. A 2001 study by the Economic and Social Research Council entitled "Willing Slaves: Employment in Britain in the 21st Century" found that "the long hours culture is more embedded for managers, those in professional jobs, and people with higher level qualifications."[iv] Similarly, the TUC has, through its Labour Force Survey, identified a marked increase in unpaid overtime among senior managers; with an average 12 hours a week of unpaid overtime, the 2006 survey saw them overtake teachers as the category of professionals with the greatest percentage of unpaid overtime. Why should it be the case that the managers and leaders towards the top of an organisation appear to be working hardest?

In addition to the fact that bosses are working long hours themselves, there is the impact of this trend on others. They are, often unwittingly, contributing to a culture in which the people that work for them also work long hours. Because they are so frenetically busy, they are often failing to find enough time to lead and manage. Delegation risks becoming a lost art as leaders fire from the hip the moment each successive message hits their BlackBerry. Not only are their people working harder, they are in all likelihood becoming progressively less effective and productive, which reduces their satisfaction in their work. And worst of all, they may be experiencing stress, something that can have a tangible physical and mental impact on not only their lives but those of their family members.

"A four day week, and then three days fun."

It appears that we have fallen into the habit of hyper-activity. We constantly check emails, send texts and make mobile phone calls – even when we are supposed to be socially engaged with others such as joining partners for a meal in a restaurant or reading our children a bed-time story. Activity is regarded as a good state and there is an unspoken stigma surrounding passive silence. Why is it, when asked if we are busy, we feel compelled to answer affirmatively?

While an entire industry has emerged offering managers life coaching, this book focuses on the work side of the equation. Drawing on the new science of evolutionary psychology, it suggests that advances in communications technology have paradoxically led us to work harder and less effectively than ever.

We start with an analysis of the problem and an understanding of the impact on working effectiveness and quality of life. I will then argue that it is the collision of two environmental factors that has caused working life to become increasingly frenetic *and* ineffective. The first of these is the technology paradox in which advances in communications technology have caused us to work harder and longer and yet less effectively than ever before; the second is the nature of human psychology which yearns for status and gossip in a world in which the traditional trappings of hierarchy have all but vanished. The combination of these two forces has led to an environment in which activity is regarded as an indicator of status, and in which the traditional Protestant work ethic has become distorted to such an extent that aggression is regarded as a pre-requisite for business success.

The book then offers practical solutions as to how some of these problems can be addressed both at a personal and an organisational level. Chapter 6 tackles the technology theme by confronting the technology paradox and offers practical tips to tame the technology beast. Chapter 7 looks at focus and how you can achieve more by taking on less. Chapter 8 examines the impact of the leader's behaviour on the rest of the organisation and how it can be coached into eradicating ineffective working practices. The following chapter covers people; the importance of having the right people in your organisation, the power of delegation and the need for effective team-working. Finally, Chapter 10 touches upon life outside the office and the personal dimension.

In addition to my academic study of organisational behaviour, this book is informed by a career of over twenty years working in companies large and small in positions ranging from junior manager to chief executive. For a two-year period, I combined a senior corporate role with being a single parent. I have not always succeeded as a manager and leader – some of the content of this book derives from lessons learned from painful experience. In my career, I have worked for and with a wide variety of managers and leaders. None has been perfect, but a small number inspired me to think hard about the way I worked and the way in which I led others. A larger number taught me only how unpleasant life can become in an organisation led by someone determined to spend every waking hour working; it's not only working life itself that can become unpleasant, since that unpleasantness inevitably bleeds into the personal lives of you and the people that work for you.

As well as contributing to stress, the impact of a long-hours culture can take the form of chronic fatigue, lack of energy and an addiction to what Dr Nick Baylis has called "emotional painkillers", be it TV, alcohol or Prozac. There is any number of ways stress can manifest itself: for me, it always seemed to break through a few days into an expensive and eagerly anticipated holiday in the form of a crippling head-cold. If you currently enjoy working in excess of sixty or seventy hours a week, then all power to you – this book is probably not for you. If, however, you recognise yourself in any of the above, read on.

This book is not about work-life balance – it is about work. It will show you that optimising your work practices and reducing your level of activity will yield benefits for both your work and personal life. Neither is it about time management – time will take care of itself and become an abundant commodity once you stop a welter of ineffective activity.

If your work is causing you to spend too little time with your family, then there is all the more reason to read this book. I have been greatly struck that the best bosses I have had in my career have been the ones that avoided a frenetic style of working, some to the point of laziness. These are the bosses from whom I have learnt the most. The result for me of their coaching and mentoring has been greater work effectiveness *and* more time with my family.

And I've yet to meet anyone in retirement who regretted that, in their working years, they spent too much time with their family.

CHAPTER ONE

Entering The Karoshi Zone

Longer Hours

In 2008, a labour office in Japan ruled the death in 2006 of a 45-year-old senior manager at Toyota to have been caused by overwork. Clinically, the cause of death was ischaemia – a shortage of blood to the heart – but the labour office ruling was 'karoshi', the Japanese word for death by overwork.

As yet, the English language does not have a word for this phenomenon, nor is there widespread evidence of the use of the Japanese word in the UK alongside more welcome imports such as sushi and teriyaki. However, there is evidence that working excessive hours is a growing problem, particularly among managers and professionals.

In a reversal of the social disparity that caused Churchill to think about leisure for the working man, the European Working Time Directive appears to have succeeded in bringing about a reduction in the average hours per week worked by men. From a peak of 45.8 hours in 1997, this has now dropped to 44.3 in 2004. However, according to research published by the TUC, the category of workers most likely to work unpaid overtime is Senior Managers who routinely work an extra 12 hours a week.[v] This appears to be a trend running counter to the overall reduction in average hours worked – the Economic and Social Research Council's Future of Work Programme of 2002 revealed that only 16 per cent of male professionals and managers said that they were completely or very satisfied with the hours they worked; this compared with 36 per cent in 1992.

How many hours should a senior manager work? This inevitably depends upon individual preference and a range of other factors. My personal view on work-rate is that after about fifty hours of work in a week, each incremental hour becomes increasingly ineffective. I had the opportunity to experience what happens at the extremes of a long-hours culture in my first job out of university, working for a leading strategy consultancy at the height of the 1980s mergers and acquisitions boom. In that environment, it was not unremarkable for young associates and consultants to work in the office through two out of three weekends; when a deadline was approaching, it was commonplace for a team to work through the night preparing a presentation or working on a financial model.

Sometimes, the long hours were an inevitable result of demands imposed by external clients that had come to the firm because of its reputation for taking on urgent projects quickly and effectively. Occasionally, however, the long hours were self-imposed, the result of a heady and occasionally self-dramatising atmosphere of my colleagues' making. Nevertheless, buoyed along by the collegiate atmosphere, I found that the contagious sense of urgency affected even me, an idle English Literature student straight out of university. Like everybody else, I scurried around in a frenzy of excitement in constant pursuit of an "urgent" piece of output.

On the occasions that I found myself having to work late into the night, I found that my reserves of energy quickly became exhausted. In spite of the contagious climate of feverish excitement and my own youthful ambition, I found myself making mistakes. By the early hours of the morning, even simple tasks such as photocopying packs of slides became thwarted by tiredness; on one occasion, an exasperated senior manager had to take the master pack from me in the early hours of the morning ahead of a presentation and re-order it.

Working for this company for a couple of years gave me an opportunity to witness what happens to people at the extremes in a high-octane, long-hours environment. I found that some of my peer group had, like me, noticed changes in temperament. Having been care-free students only months earlier, some of us now found ourselves at home some evenings weeping in front of the TV news over a third world disaster. Most people remained for two years or so and moved on, using it as a platform to a highly successful career. One or two are still there after twenty years and working as partners. Some were more resilient than others to the demands of a consistently high work-rate.

My conclusions from this early part of my career were that an individual's effectiveness at work tends to peak at a certain limit; the limit will vary – for me, as I say, it's about fifty hours per week. Work beyond this limit offers diminishing returns. If you sustain very long working hours for an extended period, it becomes harder to retain a sense of perspective. Fatigue sets in, making the individual prone to illness and depression which, even in their mildest forms, can have an impact on both professional and personal lives. For people with families, the impact is double-barrelled – firstly, work consumes the vast majority of the family member's waking hours and, secondly, the time that he or she does have with the family is tarnished by the symptoms of over-work such as tiredness and irritability.

Stress

It also appears that the nature of senior jobs is becoming more stressful, in addition to the impact of longer hours. The British Social Attitudes report into working hours published in 2007[vi] found that that professional and managerial employees were more likely to find work stressful than people in routine and manual jobs. This category is not only likely to work longer hours but is more likely to live in a household where both partners are working.

Across the whole range of employees surveyed, according to the BSA report only 8 per cent of full-time employees said they never or hardly ever find their work stressful – half the level reported in 1989. The authors of the report concluded that a "double whammy" of long hours and stress were having a negative impact on time with the family.

Further evidence of workplace stress emerged in the January 2007 survey by the Samaritans, the UK emotional support charity. The survey found that five million people are "extremely stressed" at work and that a third are taking to drink compared with just over a fifth three years ago. The problem appears to be growing with 50 per cent of respondents saying that they felt more stressed in 2006 than they had five years earlier. The Samaritans' research echoes findings elsewhere that the problem is more acute with senior managers and professionals. Some segments, such as civil servants, report 70 per cent feeling more stress than five years earlier.

This is entirely understandable in the context of the twenty-first century workplace. Stress is a healthy and necessary human response which, in the ancestral environment, drove us to either confront whatever threatened us or avoid the threat altogether. Avoidance could take the form of submission by acknowledging higher status in a conflict situation; alternatively, it could take the form of simply escaping the situation altogether. This is the "fight or flight" response. Today's working environment is altogether different and rarely, if ever, the source of immediate physical threat. The source of our stress in today's organisation is more likely to be an over-flowing in-box from which, thanks to mobile communications technology, there is no escape.

We shall come to why communications technology has become a cause of stress rather than a solution. The latest technology, while introduced with the intention of increasing productivity, can often be counter-productive due to its ubiquity and ease of use. It is not uncommon for people at all levels in the hierarchy to receive as many as two hundred emails a day. With senior managers emailing across the weekend, even time out of the office is tinged with the consciousness of the accumulating emails awaiting a return to work. The prospect of an in-box overflowing with thousands of emails inevitably casts a shadow over a fortnight's holiday. As we shall see, in some companies such a prospect is enough to put some people off taking a holiday at all. The ubiquity and remorselessness of electronic communication is a significant source of stress because there is no escape and the only way to confront it is to work through it, however long it takes.

As long ago as the 1920s, psychologists such as Walter B. Cannon asserted that in addition to having short-term effects, stress can have a long-term impact, such as causing disease. In today's office, while there is neither fight nor flight in the traditional sense with sources of stress being far less tangible, the fact remains that stress is ubiquitous in a way that was not the case in the ancestral environment. While there remains a vigorous debate among psychologists and physicians as to the precise relationship between stress and illness, there are inevitable consequences for health. Work psychologists Stephen Barley and Deborah Knight suggest that the manifestations of stress include: "the occurrence of unpleasant and potentially unhealthy psychological, physical and behavioral symptoms such as diffuse anxiety, chronic irritability, insomnia and elevated serum cholesterol counts." [vii]

Reduced Effectiveness at Work

In addition to being unpleasant in its own right and contributing to illness, stress also reduces effectiveness at work. The Samaritans' "Stressed Out" survey reports that 21 per cent of respondents feel that they are not as efficient at work as normal as a result of stress. Other manifestations of stress include:

"I feel more irritable than usual" (68 per cent)

"My sleep pattern is disturbed" (56 per cent)

"I find it hard to concentrate" (33 per cent)

"I am more forgetful than normal" (32 per cent)[viii]

This suggests that cognitive functioning, memory and concentration are all diminished by stress. This inevitably has consequences for the individual's effectiveness at work, none more so than for those in leadership roles. If this is evident in you as a leader, irritability will be evident among the people that work for you, making them feel more defensive and less comfortable about raising issues openly. It will undermine one of the key roles of the leader in communicating to his or her organisation confidence in direction and progress. A tired and drawn leader will cause speculation within the organisation as to what might be wrong; the ensuing gossip will raise anxiety and serve as a distraction.

Reduced concentration has a negative impact on decision-making and can lead to mistakes. If the brain's analytical functions are impaired, it will be harder for a manager or leader to deliver on one of their most important roles – to offer perspective and a more considered view than that apparent to staff members immersed in day-to-day issues.

An impaired short-term memory makes it more likely that mistakes will be made, ultimately increasing further the workload for you and your team. It also means having to re-read documents or replay conversations with staff because you've failed to retain the information that you derived on the first pass. As well as being inefficient, this can reduce levels of confidence among your staff who do not feel you are retaining what they tell you. If agreements in meetings or discussions are also forgotten, this can lead to the appearance of failing to honour something.

Poor sleep patterns will increase the prevalence of the other symptoms, leading to a vicious cycle in which stress is increased, in turn causing sleep to be disrupted still further.

At extreme levels, work-related stress causes mental health issues and I have seen examples in companies with particularly pressurised working environments of individuals developing severe problems. Even at a more mundane level, however, the impact of stress on effectiveness at work can be significant, both on the individual and the people that work for them. We have all found ourselves in situations where a difficult spell at work causes stress levels to increase with consequential lapses in short-term memory and increases in irritability. In addition to making the work environment less pleasant for everybody, the likelihood is that effectiveness will be reduced, mistakes will be made and less will be achieved.

Impact on Family Life

The British Social Attitudes survey published in January 2007 showed the extent to which people now feel that work is encroaching on family life. Of full-time men, 69 per cent and of full-time women, 58 per cent, say that the demands of their job interfere with their family life at least sometimes. Only 29 per cent of full-time men and 19 per cent of full-time women say that the demands of family life rarely interfere with their work.

So there is clearly a level of interference here. But even where managers and leaders are with their families, is there a reduction in the quality of that time? Certainly, if the manifestations of stress such as irritability and tiredness pollute domestic life then there is a real risk that people will simply be too busy and stressed to give their families their full attention. Some of the additional manifestations of stress that will have an impact on the family include:

- I have more arguments with my partner.
- My sex life suffers.
- I don't spend enough quality time with my children.

For an illustration – albeit an extreme one - of how the stress of work can impact the family, rent the film *Kidulthood* and watch out for the middle class father so tied up in his work that he fails to realise the suicidal state of his teenage daughter. The rash of teenage killings in February 2007 sparked a wide-ranging debate about the role of parents with particular emphasis on the need to force absent parents to play a larger role in the life of their children. This is not an issue limited to the "underclass" or lower socio-demographic groups: among professional parents, particularly where both are working full time, there is a need to ensure not only that adequate time is spent with children, but also that that time is of a sufficiently high quality. The term "BlackBerry orphan" has taken hold in the US to describe children whose time with their parents is blighted by their parents' constant checking for messages. *The Wall Street Journal* in December 2006 featured the drastic response of one Texan seven-year old that claimed to have tried to flush her mother's device down the toilet.[ix]

Tackling Stress and its Consequences

Businesses are becoming more concerned about overwork and stress, not least because of union activity and fear of legal action. Other agencies have also become involved. Sadly, action is all too often either gimmicky or superficial and does not address root causes.

From the charity sector, the Samaritans have become so concerned about stress that, in addition to commissioning research on the subject, they have launched Stress Down Day as a fund- and awareness-raising exercise. The first national Stress Down Day took place on 1st February 2007 and employees were urged to arrive for work wearing slippers as a light-hearted way to make the point. While clearly well-intentioned, exercises such as this can have only limited impact. Where stress is an issue in a company's workforce, it is really something the leadership of that company has to tackle. All too often, however, leaders respond to stress as something that is up to the individual to control. As Barley and Knight wrote in 1992:

"Even more felicitous for management may be the intimation that stress is primarily an individual problem: a failure to cope. By legitimating concern over stress and by providing opportunities to learn "coping strategies," organizations countenance the perception that individuals are partially, if not wholly, to blame for their own predicament. Thus, the tenor of most stress management programs subtly draws attention away from conditions of work and refocuses it on the individual's weaknesses and anxieties while signalling the organization's apparent concern for the employee's welfare."

My more recent experience confirms this to be the case. I have seen a few corporate attempts to deal with stress among employees, as the issue is often one of the most prominent ones raised in employee satisfaction surveys. Never have I seen a heartfelt commitment to changing the cultural and behavioural causes at the root of the problem which is, after all, situational. Instead, the problem becomes, along with all others exposed by internal employee satisfaction surveys, delegated to a hapless human resources department as part of an employee satisfaction "action plan". Components of the stress action plan that I have seen typically include initiatives such as:

- distribution of small branded rubber balls that employees can squeeze to reduce stress
- funding of masseurs to give free head massages during employees' breaks
- two-hour presentations from stress consultants at team away-days.

Inevitably, these barely scratch the surface of the problem and leave the individual disillusioned and cynical about the organisation.

The last Government also became involved in the issue, partnering a number of employers to form an alliance, Employers for Work-Life Balance, to promote the benefits of work-life balance to the business community. In June 2000, it even launched a Work-Life Balance Challenge Fund "which provides consultancy advice to businesses to help them examine working practices and business objectives and introduce changes to benefit both their business and their employees". Is there a role for Government in this issue, particularly from one that, from the Prime Minister down, was open to accusations of having led over a decade of frenzied activity for negligible achievements?

One force for change that has had some positive impact has been what has broadly been described as "flexibility". This involves exploiting communications technology to allow people to work at times and locations that suit them. This can alleviate a difficult commute or make space for other activities without having a negative impact on work. In many companies, some staff members have been migrated to "homeworker" status.

For many individuals, flexibility can reduce some of the aspects of work that are most stressful. However, it does not work for everybody for a number of reasons. Firstly, not everybody has the right domestic environment for home-working. For anyone that does not have a study in which they can shut themselves away, they risk disruption at work, particularly if there are young children in the house. Also, they need discipline to ensure that they are not working late into the night, risking a degradation of the sanctity of their domestic environment. If this happens, they risk work bleeding into home life, making it more difficult to switch off and resist stress.

Another danger lies in the way employers are tempted to see flexibility as a cost-reduction opportunity. Technology has liberated employers from having to provide staff with a dedicated desk and PC; it is now possible for an employee to be armed with a laptop and the technology to "touch down" at any "workstation" and be able to work effectively. One company I worked for, noting that employees were on average working two days each week from home, converted an entire open plan office into "hot desks" with only three desks for every four employees. "Hot desks" were so called because they were no longer assigned to individuals – you now had to find a free desk at which to plug in your laptop and work. There was no longer a place for personal photos or other items. Inevitably, there were far too few "hot desks", with the result that employees had to get into the office increasingly early to be sure of getting one. Instead of the working day starting at 9.00, one of the unintended consequences of the "flexible" approach was that by 8.00 each morning, the office was already crowded. This factor, combined with the drastic reduction in personal offices for senior managers (up to and including people reporting directly to the Group Chief Executive) meant that everybody, from the divisional Managing Director right down to the most junior administrator, had to work out of one large open plan office. The intentions behind the initiative were good as it was hoped that the move would make the organisation less hierarchical and facilitate greater communication. However, since people were no longer allocated fixed phones, everybody took calls on their mobile, frequently pacing the floor around them and shouting as they did so. People were not only forced to get in early in order to get a desk, but they also felt pressured to remain in the office later.

Another unintended consequence of open plan offices is that, because everybody is so visible to one another, "presenteeism" has set in. A YouGov poll for Microsoft published in November 2006 found that 53 per cent of respondents felt that the open plan office was the most significant change in office life. Longer working hours was

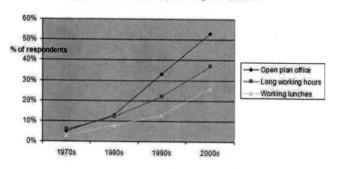

Characteristics of the office through the decades

Source: YouGov, November 2006

second at 37 per cent. There is a clear correlation between the two (see the graph below), suggesting that the open plan office has been a contributing factor in the growth in working hours.

Human beings are wonderfully adaptive animals and, to some extent, we have become inured to the way we live and work, but how did we get to this position when a generation ago we were on the threshold of an age of leisure? Part of the answer is our use of technological advancements in our working lives – what were envisaged as tools to liberate us have ended up enslaving us.

CHAPTER TWO

"Email is Ruining My Life" (Part One)

Where is the wisdom we have lost in knowledge?
Where is the knowledge we have lost in information?
T.S.Eliot (1888-1965) The Rock, 1936

In 2008, the BBC broadcast a Money Programme special titled "Email is ruining my life." The programme asserted that a third of office workers suffer from email stress; Professor Cary Cooper of Lancaster University cited email as one of the greatest stressors of modern working life. The programme portrayed an "email-addicted" businesswoman who left her BlackBerry on by her bed-side all night buzzing with each inbound message, disturbing sleep for her and her partner.

In 2009, France Telecom – the national telephony operator in a country with a reputation for a relaxed approach to work – became embroiled in a crisis sparked by a spate of employee suicides. While not directly attributing the suicides to email, the company's CFO, Gervais Pellissier, cited overwhelming volumes of email and the pervasive nature of PDAs as a major contributor to the stress experienced by the company's employees: "Today for people working in business, whatever the level, whether they are CEO or even first- or second-rank level employees, they are always connected."[x]

Huge advances have been made in communications technology over recent decades and I am not suggesting for a moment that it would be better if we could turn the clock back and "un-invent" them. Nevertheless, for a number of reasons, we risk becoming enslaved by a series of work innovations that, paradoxically, were introduced in order to ease life at the office.

Table 1 compares the number of communications media available now compared with 25 years ago. This is a period that happens to straddle my own experience of office life since, in 1985, I took on a holiday job in the London office of Chase Manhattan bank writing user manuals for their early electronic banking software packages. This required me to sit at a desk using word-processing software on a desktop computer (both recent innovations at the time) with my fixed telephone extension as the only voice communications device.

What is evident about the 2010 column is that not only has the range of communications media expanded significantly, so too has their mobility. Mobility has been transformed by the dual advances in computing and mobile communications technology; not only have the fixed phone and desktop computer been liberated from the office, they have even been combined into one pocket-sized device. These advances mean a) that we have a significantly increased number of channels via which we can contact and be contacted, and b) that we no longer have any temporal or geographical constraints on their use.

1985	*2010*
Telephone call (fixed)	Telephone call (fixed)
Post	Post
Face-to-face	Face-to-face contact
	Telephone call (mobile)
	Email
	SMS
	Instant Message
	Social Media (LinkedIn, Facebook, Twitter)

Table 1. The growth in contact channels 1985-2010. Bold signifies temporal and location independence.

In 1985 it was possible to be interrupted by a phone call on the fixed extension, by the delivery to your in-tray of some internal or external post or by a colleague walking up to your desk. If I were writing that user-manual today, I would have the additional possibilities of receiving:

- a call on my mobile
- a text message
- a desktop alert on my computer indicating a new email
- an Instant Message popping up on my computer.

I have excluded for the purposes of this exercise the incoming messages from social networking sites. If I were using a laptop rather than a desktop computer and chose to take my work away to my home or on holiday, all of the new, incremental channels above would travel with me.

This explosion in the number of contact channels, combined with their mobility, has major implications for twenty-first century working life. While there are a number of enormous positives associated with the advances in technology, there are also some problems, three of which are core problems: 1) the sheer volume of email messages, many of them irrelevant to the recipient; 2) the impact on work effectiveness caused by interruption from the various new contact channels; and 3) the perceived "addiction" to email, particularly through the use of "Personal Digital Assistants" (PDAs) such as the BlackBerry. Let's take each of these three in turn.

1. The cost of excessive email volume

The most obvious manifestation of the problem with email is simply volume. We get too much of it – more than we can reasonably be expected to stay on top of. Some companies have published internal surveys of employees' perceptions of email volumes. While working at Intel, Nathan Zeldes, President of the Information Overload Research Group, found in a company-wide survey conducted in March 2006 that employees received an average of 350 work-related emails every week. Surveying the company's sales and marketing function later that year he found the average weekly number to be 400.[xi]

My personal experience is that this number is often much higher, reaching the low hundreds *daily* for many managers and leaders. One of the paradoxes of modern working life – that the more senior you get, the harder you have to work – appears anecdotally to be borne out by email volumes. Some leaders will have their PAs manage the bulk of their emails, but the advent of BlackBerrys means that many choose to stay in personal control of their in-box.

Spiralling email volumes are partly a result of the way we use the medium. I would argue that email is the perfect channel for distributing non-urgent information to multiple recipients quickly. However, the way we react to it means that all messages become treated as urgent. Tom Jackson of

Loughborough University conducted some research into email response behaviours among employees at Darnwood Group, a retailer of office solutions. He found that 70 per cent of emails were opened within six seconds and that 85 per cent of emails were opened within two minutes of arriving.[xii] There are a variety of reasons why we might choose to pounce on each email as it comes in, some of which we will come to later. If we work in an environment where email *is* used for urgent communication, by leaving a new message unopened, we may be failing in the performance of our job. It may also be easier to see what the new message is rather than continue with the existing task – in other words, opening the new email is a form of task avoidance. Simplest of all, until we open the message, we don't know what it contains – it could be anything from a juicy bit of gossip to news about someone being fired. Our curiosity inevitably gets the better of us and we open the message.

The simple fact is that, based on Tom Jackson's research, we do treat email as an urgent – possibly the most urgent – form of communication. Six seconds is, after all, as Jackson points out, less than it takes for a phone to ring three times. Having opened the message, of course, we often feel compelled to reply to show that we are on the case, perhaps using to "reply-to-all" to communicate this to everyone to whom the first message was distributed. In this way, message volumes spiral upwards.

The issue of email volume alone is a very significant contributor to the problem of ineffective and unhealthy working practices. The constant accumulation of messages causes unyielding pressure on the individual to tackle the overload not just at work but while away from the office, even on holiday. When an individual is close to being overwhelmed by their in-box, they lose sight of what messages need to be dealt with. Tactics in these circumstances include forwarding emails to oneself so that messages that need dealing with appear – at least momentarily – as unread messages at the top of the in-box. In cases of extreme volumes, there is the concept for personal messages of "email bankruptcy" in which defeat is admitted and the entire in-box is deleted. According to research conducted by AOL in 2008, 27 per cent of respondents had already "declared" themselves bankrupt (i.e. they had zapped the contents of their in-box) or were seriously thinking about doing so.[xiii] In a work environment, this would be unthinkable; nevertheless, it is increasingly the case in corporates that staff simply ignore messages that are not from their boss; this is email bankruptcy in all but name.

In addition to the sheer volume of email, there is the issue of work-related email that contributes nothing to the recipient's execution of their job. It might be a message copied unnecessarily that requires a few minutes' reading before it can be designated as irrelevant. It could equally be a "reply-to-all" message that really did not need to include all original recipients. Whatever their origin, unproductive work-related emails soak up a significant amount of time and energy. Christina Cavanagh's research at the University of Toronto quantifies the impact of this as equivalent to 12 per cent of a company's payroll.[xiv] Nathan Zeldes's employee-wide survey at Intel found that 30 per cent of incoming messages were perceived as unnecessary and that it took two of the 20 hours they spent each week on email to process them.

2. The cost of interruptions

If we return briefly to Table 1, we can use it to visualise a working day in which a typical worker might be making progress on a piece of output, be it a tender document, a financial model or a report for a presentation to senior management. All of these should ultimately have a commercial impact for the employer as they will result in the winning of business or contribute to the decision-making process. If the worker sets aside the morning to work on the project in question, he or she could be interrupted via all of the channels listed. The nature and frequency of the interruption will depend upon settings and options the worker has chosen. The arrival of each email might be announced by one or all of the following: 1) a noise; 2) the appearance of an envelope in the notification area; 3) change in the shape of the mouse cursor on the screen; or 4) a desktop alert showing the first few lines of the message.

The negative impact of this level of interruption is a known fact. Research conducted by Pitney Bowes into the experience of knowledge workers in 1998 suggested that they received on average six interruptions every hour of the working day.[xv] O'Conaill and Frohlich's work in 1995 showed that managers spent 10 minutes of each working hour dealing with interruptions and that 41 per cent of the time they did not return to the original task.[xvi] Thomas Jackson's research at Loughborough showed that, where they did return to the original task, it took office workers 64 seconds to fully recover their thoughts. What psychologists tell us is that interruptions generate two different types of interference. Capacity interference occurs when the number of incoming requests for our attention is greater than our capacity to deal with them. This might take the form of a colleague at our shoulder, an incoming SMS message and a bleep indicating a new email all happening at once. Structural interference takes place when the brain is required to manage two inputs that require the same physiological mechanism. An example is looking at a document on a computer and reading the preview of the email that pops up at the bottom of the screen. These types of interference result in a drain on our cognitive processing resources, leading to reduced performance; this might take the form of short-term memory loss or confusion. It is capacity interference that is at work when a poor presenter puts up Powerpoint slides loaded with text – and then reads the text to the hapless audience; the impact on the brain is a doubling of the demands placed on its processing power, which often results in the audience member falling asleep. It is worth making the observation here that if, in Microsoft Outlook, you accept the default setting of all four types of email alert, you are exposing yourself to both capacity and channel interference simultaneously. It is as if the package were designed to maximise the detrimental impact on the user's brain.

Research by business psychologists has shown that interruptions have a much greater detrimental impact on our cognitive ability than is commonly thought. Also, the more complex the task, the greater the negative impact from interruptions on our ability to complete it. As well as taking longer to complete the task, we are more likely to make mistakes, take short-cuts or start to feel stressed.

A striking illustration of the impact interruptions have on our cognitive ability is offered by the research conducted by Glenn Wilson, a psychologist from King's College London into IQ levels in eight subjects who were asked questions and given challenges while new emails were dropped into their in-boxes. Wilson carried out 80 clinical trials and found an average reduction in IQ of ten points; the research, prepared on behalf of Hewlett Packard, was compared by the company's publicists Porter-Novelli to studies of cannabis users that identified a four-point reduction in IQ. Wilson himself distanced himself from the comparison, which was not entirely valid from a research perspective. However, it is repeated frequently in recurring press coverage.[xvii]

What is the cost of the twin productivity leeches of email overload and multi-channel interruption? From his work at Intel, Nathan Zeldes estimates two hours per week is lost through processing unnecessary email. As regards interruptions, he has performed detailed calculations that account for the time lost from the interruption and the recovery time needed to return to the original task. Using published research, he assumes that three interruptions per hour are received – this is 50 per cent of what the research suggests, but the figure has been halved in order to be conservative. He then builds in results of published work on typical work sequences and assumes an eight-minute task performed without interruptions becomes a twelve-minute task following an interruption. Allowance is also made for the fact the original task is often forgotten. Zeldes's conclusion is that six hours per week is lost as a result of interruptions. In aggregate this is eight hours or one fifth of a 40-hour working week. Some allowance must be made for the fact employees will often work longer hours in order to compensate for lost time, but this in itself reduces effectiveness and brings with it additional problems such as stress. Even if the 20 per cent were only

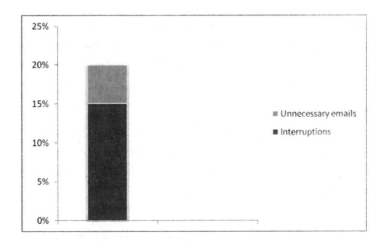

Table 2. The cost of interruptions and unnecessary email.

half true, it suggests a vast avoidable cost to the employer.

Zeldes is not alone in his findings. In 2005 Microsoft surveyed 38,000 people across 200 countries in their Personal Productivity Challenge research exercise. With respondents working an average of 45 hours per week, they viewed an average of 17 of those hours as unproductive, with 55 per cent directly relating their productivity issues to information technology.[xviii]

In short, we have multiplied the number of communication channels we use at work and vastly increased their mobility; yet, our physiological processing equipment evolved in our ancestral environment where there were far fewer sources of interruption and lower volumes of messages. One innovation in particular appears to have outstripped our mental ability to handle it – the PDA or BlackBerry.

CHAPTER THREE

"Email Is Ruining My Life" (Part Two): "Addiction Is A Choice"

What hath God wrought?
(Samuel Morse in the world's first telegraph message, 1844)

For a great personal illustration of the so-called addictiveness of the BlackBerry – one of a number of devices used for managing email on the move - read this extract of an open "letter" written by Adam Bryant to his jettisoned device and published in the *New York Times* in June 2006:

"Dear BlackBerry

It's been a few weeks since we parted company. I'm sure you've forgotten me by now and are still hard at work for my former employer.

That's good. No hard feelings. I've decided I'm actually better off without you.

Why? Because even though you made me feel more productive, I'm realising that in fact you made me less so.

You were always tugging at my sleeve, your blinking red light a constant reminder that maybe, just maybe, you had an urgent e-mail for me. You were a black hole of attention. If there was something urgent, I reasoned, better to know about it sooner rather than later. So I checked. And checked."[xix]

Bryant goes on to fantasise about a "BlackBerry blackout" that would "strengthen marriages and friendships". While written in a tongue-in-cheek manner, the description of the impulse to keep checking will, I suspect, evoke a smile of recognition among all BlackBerry-armed executives.

But while Bryant's letter was written tongue-in-cheek, there is increasing awareness of the detrimental impact of continuous BlackBerry use on life outside work, something that affects even the most successful CEOs. Interviewed in August 2009 in the *Sunday Telegraph*, Aidan Heavey – founder and chief executive of Tullow Oil – was asked when he last took a holiday:

"It's all work. I don't relax. Haven't you heard of a thing called a BlackBerry?... I can't turn off. I look at my BlackBerry every 10 seconds. I check it when I'm going up in ski lifts and drive my playing partners mad by answering emails on the golf course. They're the best and worst invention ever. They mean that you work 24 hours a day and you don't get holidays. They've changed life."[xx]

This phenomenon has been researched by Professor Nada Kakabadse of Northampton University. In June 2009, she told *The Times:* ""From my research, you'd be surprised how many people had their BlackBerry next to their beds. They would pick up messages two or three times a night. It certainly created friction in some of the relationships of the people I spoke to. In some cases it led to divorce when one partner felt the other wasn't paying enough attention to normal human interaction."[xxi] The demise of the marriage between Madonna and Guy Ritchie may have been hastened by their habit of keeping BlackBerrys under their pillows. "It's not unromantic" she said when asked about the practice. "It's practical." Six months later, the couple separated.

American email provider AOL has been running its annual "Email Addiction Survey" for four years and found in its 2008 survey that 46 per cent of 4000 respondents categorised themselves as "hooked" on email; the issue seems to have got more acute over time since the 2007 figure was just 15 per cent – perhaps a function of the fact that 55 per cent of respondents had upgraded to a new mobile device in the past year in order to get emails on the move. Particularly worrying for the way in which work increasingly eats into personal time, 62 per cent of respondents said they check work emails over a typical weekend with 19 per cent doing so five or more times. 28 per cent checked work email while on holiday. The survey asked respondents to acknowledge some of the various places from which they checked emails on mobile devices:

- In bed in their pyjamas: 67 per cent
- From the bathroom: 59 per cent (up from 53 per cent last year)
- While driving: 50 per cent (up from 37 per cent last year)
- In a bar or club: 39 per cent
- In a business meeting: 38 per cent
- During happy hour: 34 per cent
- While on a date: 25 per cent
- From church: 15 per cent (up from 12 per cent last year).

Why is it that what should be regarded as labour-saving technology can end up reducing our effectiveness at work and, indeed, "ruining our lives"? Why is that we focus on a device as the cause of "addiction" and misery? The answer lies partly in the nature not of the technology itself, but in human psychology. First of all, however, there is a need to address the concept that those, like Adam Bryant, who feel chained to their BlackBerrys are experiencing "addiction".

The Addiction Myth

Addiction is a liberating concept as it both medicalises and externalises the problem of habituation to a substance or behaviour be it cocaine, alcohol, gambling, sex or BlackBerry usage. By presenting the problem to oneself and others as an "addiction", the behaviour becomes less a voluntary activity for which one is personally responsible and more a sickness that takes hold with an unshakeable grip. There are some that take this view even with hard drugs. In his book *Addiction is a Choice*, Jeffrey A. Schaler[xxii] rejects the disease model of drug abuse for the very reason that it absolves the individual of personal responsibility. He makes the point that individuals with chronic drug problems *can* change their behaviour, but it requires them to genuinely want to change. He suggests that prevailing drug policies revolve around the medical assumption that hard drugs establish an inexorable grip upon users that cannot be shaken off. There is evidence of whole cohorts of users that manage to shrug off their use, particularly when they change their environment; Schaler cites US troops returning from Vietnam as an example.

Even if one does not take this hard-line view, it is difficult to regard habitual use of the BlackBerry in the same vein as that of a hard drug. After all, while addiction as a condition is being applied to an increasingly broad range of behavior, it is generally used in the context of a chronic neurobiological disorder.

Some research equates the experience of receiving email to that of gambling. Dr Tom Stafford, a lecturer at the University of Sheffield says: "Both slot machines and email follow something called a 'variable interval reinforcement schedule' which has been established as the way to train in the strongest habits. This means that rather than reward an action every time it is performed, you reward it sometimes, but not in a predictable way. So with email - usually when I check it there is nothing interesting, but every so often there's something wonderful – an invite out, or maybe some juicy gossip – and I get a reward."[xxiii]

It is significant that Dr Stafford refers to gossip as this is something to which we shall return. But the concept of email as a "reward" suggests a physiological process that drives behaviour in helpless adults – something Schaler rejects. As he says himself: "Chemical rewards have no power to compel - although this notion of compulsion may be a cherished part of clinicians' folklore. I am rewarded every time I eat chocolate cake, but I often eschew this reward because I feel I ought to watch my weight."

Nevertheless, the concept of BlackBerry addiction has taken hold, with the result that the device has been nick-named the "Crackberry". Indeed, it is possible to take a "twelve-step" approach to so-called BlackBerry addiction, something offered by a number of consultants such as

Marsha Egan in the US. She has cited the example of a golfing client who checked his BlackBerry after every shot and lost a potential customer who thought he was a socially-inept obsessive. The "twelve-step" approach advocated for alcoholics by Alcoholics Anonymous insists on complete abstention, while Schaler takes the view that moderation is entirely possible. In the context of technology I also argue against abstention, as email and BlackBerry remain important tools. We shall come later in the book to how to moderate usage of these tools in order to heighten personal effectiveness. But at this point let us distance ourselves from the idea that there is an implacable physiological process at play with email compulsion; let us look instead at some of the psychological drivers. Looking at the issue in this way, we will see that there are two initial causes behind our suffering from technology overload (we will come to other contributory factors shortly):

- the technology is available
- it fulfills a fundamental human need for gossip.

1) Availability
It may seem a mundane point but the very availability of communications technology is itself a driver of increased activity. Prior to the widespread use of email in the 1990s, there were very real practical limits to office-based activity and communication. A symbol of this in my mind is a

defunct box that sat in the lobby of an office I once worked in until the building was demolished in the 1990s. The box invited you to put in documents for typing by 3pm in order to get back a proof by the end of the next working day.

So, a paper document took a whole day to get typed up and required checking and editing and copying; then it would be distributed by internal post. It might be three days before a communiqué of this sort reached the recipient. It may sound like a ritual from the Stone Age but was common practice as recently as the late 1980s. To the twenty-first century manager, this process appears frustratingly slow but, paradoxically, it did have benefits: not least of these was that managers and leaders had to be sparing about the thoughts or instructions they committed to writing. Urgent matters were dealt with via a phone call or a face-to-face conversation. If an individual was out of the office, he or she would have a well-briefed subordinate to handle any issues. Many messages of course would simply not have happened at all – with the passage of time, the query might have been answered or simply become overtaken by events.

Thus, part of the problem with the volume of communication is its ease of use. Email is instant and, with the arrival of BlackBerrys and GPRS, universally available almost regardless of time and location. The most direct impact of this technology is that it enables people to work limitless hours. If an executive is not on the receiving end of a sufficient number of emails and phone calls, the best possible way to change this is to stimulate some by creating as many as possible themselves. We shall come to what is driving the desire to do this.

This immediacy and availability is a powerful driver of use that is easy to overlook. I think of it in the same terms as the way the high suicide rate among vets is often rationalised – social isolation, the cumulative impact of dealing with bereaved pet owners, the stress of putting down animals, and so on. But why should this drive a suicide rate that is, according to research by the British Veterinary Association, four times the national average? It is also twice that of other professionals such as doctors (many of whom face arguably more stressful situations around human terminal illness and death) and dentists. Part of the answer lies in the readily available quantities of drugs such as horse-tranquilisers not matched in other professions. As Dr Virginia Richmond of the Veterinary Surgeons Health Support Programme put it, "It's sitting there on the shelves looking at them."

Rather than taking industrial quantities of ketamine, modern professionals use information technology partly for the simple reason that it is available and easy to use. Email has liberated administrators from the laborious task of distributing mundane paper memos to staff. However, the technology now makes it possible to send an email with such rapidity that messages often go out without the author having had an opportunity to think deeply about the content, quality or audience. The "reply-to-all" function of email means that, with a few key-strokes, any of the recipients can generate another email, copying in more colleagues if necessary. Anyone perceiving the slightest criticism in an email is naturally prompted to respond. And in this way, long chain emails can snowball to the extent that people become immersed in the electronic debate. The inevitable results of a culture of high-volume shooting-from-the-hip email are a) reduced organisational effectiveness and b) an increase in the volume of work.

A walk around almost any open-plan office will demonstrate the prevalence of the problem with most people staring at their email in-boxes, held captive as if in some form of email jail. The immediacy of email and the direct personal nature of the messaging means that many people find themselves tethered to their computers by this invisible chain. As the volume of email increases, they find it harder and harder to deal effectively with their burgeoning in-box, often opening and closing the same item many times over as they try to find a way to deal with it. For many without very immediate tangible objectives such as sales targets, sitting at their email in-box *becomes* their job, and it is indeed a form of activity that requires little thought or self-discipline. The problem with this is that it gives them less time to do their actual job and deliver against objectives and so the volume of work goes up. A large survey in 2003 by the Australian Psychological Society found that 80 per cent of workers spent more than 20 per cent of their day dealing with emails.[xxiv]

BlackBerrys and other PDAs have had such an impact because they take all the aspects of email that stimulate extra communication and then add the facility of doing so on the move. The impact is one of huge additional stimulation. Where people waiting alone on a train platform might once have eased the pressures of solitude by lighting a cigarette, they can now make a phone call or, more likely still, send some emails.

2) The Fundamental Human Need for Gossip

What we are beginning to establish is that it is not the technology here that is of itself addictive; rather, it is a number of human needs such as wanting to be part of the action and in on the important discussions.

It is at this point helpful to introduce the study of evolutionary psychology as it can throw light upon human behaviour in the workplace. Broadly speaking, humans are "wired" in much the same way as our hunter–gatherer ancestors were as much as 100,000 years ago when their environment was nomadic, and their community was limited to bands of about 150. Outsiders to the band posed an immediate physical threat and would have been viewed with initial hostility. Leadership within the band was complex in its nature and prone to change depending upon a number of factors; these included the level of perceived support that potential leadership rivals could discern among other band members.

The environment of our ancestors and their development as social animals with the capacity for language in many ways determined the way we are today. Evolutionary theory is hotly debated among psychologists and is often derided as comprising of little more than "Just So" stories since – in the absence of the ability to conduct controlled experiments – there is often little evidence available beyond supposition.

Nevertheless, there is a wealth of compelling writing on evolutionary psychology, although almost none on its application to the work environment. An exception is psychologist Nigel Nicholson, author of *Managing the Human Animal*[xxv], who has additionally written in the *Journal of Organizational Behavior* on why evolutionary theory is so poorly utilised by the work psychology community.

The urge to gossip, then, is a natural human desire that, like the importance of social status, which we shall come to, has its roots in our ancestral environment. Here is Robert Wright in *The Moral Animal*[xxvi] on the importance of information exchange in the ancestral environment:

"Knowing where a great stock of food has been found, or where someone encountered a poisonous snake, can be a matter of life or death. And knowing who is sleeping with whom, who is angry with whom, who cheated whom and so on, can inform social manoeuvering for sex and other vital resources."

Indeed, social psychologist Nicholas Emler[xxvii], speaking at the 2009 British Science Festival, identified gossip as one of the reasons we as humans can live in much larger social groups than other primates – baboons and chimps, not having language, need to rely on direct observation to form opinions about one another, and this drives an upper limit on group size of about 50. For humans, the number is larger. We will come to what this number is and the implications for organisation at work.

Emler's research includes a study of 300 volunteers in which he quantified the nature of their interactions with one another. He found that nearly 80 per cent of their interactions with other people consisted of sharing social information. He concludes that the activity must have been fundamental to the development of humans otherwise we would not invest so much time in it.

While in the ancestral environment, accrual of this sort of information ultimately contributed to survival and reproduction, in the modern corporate environment it is more about politics: who is in and who is out, rumoured reorganisations and so on. When thinking of gossip in the organisational context, it is a mistake to regard it in its everyday caricature sense as the pursuit of fish-wives or as a principally female activity. As Nigel Nicholson writes in *Managing the Human Animal*, it tends to pursue what is very much a "male agenda" incorporating valuable nuggets of information he describes in figurative terms such as "status-checking, cast-listing, weather forecasting, line-laying and grooming."

We are able to expand our social groups beyond the 50 or so that other closely-related primates can manage because we use gossip from others as shorthand. This is why reputations can be built or destroyed by what others say about an individual. The need to rely on information gleaned from others because of the large volume of individuals we encounter also makes sense when one considers other manifestations of our tendency to categorise new individuals very rapidly based on the first pieces of information we receive about them, whether directly or otherwise. This is why the truism "first impressions last" tends to hold true; for all the science and psychological profiling behind modern recruitment processes, we too frequently rationalise decisions based upon those key initial pieces of data.

In an office environment, this exchange of information among senior managers once took the form of corridor chats or discreet drinks at lunchtime in the corner of the pub. Now, technology has liberated the exchange of information to the extent that it can take place over the airwaves regardless of time or location. Furthermore, unless one is physically at the same location as all managers of consequence, there is no knowing when the next significant email will hit the in-box, hence the need to check constantly. Research suggests that we practically pounce on every new message; this is illustrated by Tom Jackson's findings that we pounce on our new email messages within six seconds.

So why does this compulsion to check each incoming email still feel like an addiction? Some light has been thrown on this by the contributions of University of Texas neuroscientist Russell Poldrack to the Huffington Post[xxviii]. He makes the point that dopamine, the chemical sent out by the brain system, is activated by novelty. The brain rewards itself when new events or facts are noticed. As Poldrack points out: "This makes a lot sense from an evolutionary standpoint, since we don't want to spend all our time and energy noticing the many things that don't change from day to day." Poldrack describes dopamine as the "gimme more" neurotransmitter – in addition to novelty, the dopamine system is also stimulated by drugs that create euphoria such as cocaine and methamphetamine. The opioid system within the brain – the one that is associated with euphoria – is very closely linked to the dopamine system. So the behaviours associated with drugs are closely related to those we recognise around email and PDAs. But it is the evolutionary hunger for new information that drives us to check constantly for each incoming message.

The checking impulse is not limited to BlackBerrys and PDAs. We also check constantly when at our desktop computers and working on other tasks. This was demonstrated by Karen Renaud[xxix], Judith Ramsay and Mario Hair in their 2006 study of Glasgow University academics, researchers and support staff, during which they conducted a detailed investigation of desktop email behaviours. They found that in the average session hour, users switched between applications 36 times. The average time they spent on email each time they switched was 47 seconds, with 56.5 per cent of email sessions lasting less than 15 seconds. This, the authors say, suggests "users were simply checking their e-mail without acting on it". Further research in the same paper suggests that this switching behaviour occurs even when alerts for new emails are switched off. So even without external interruptions, we often disrupt our own work because of this compulsion to check.

Furthermore, we are driven by anxiety about how we are perceived in the digital community. Instead of our ancestral band of 150, the digital community is unlimited. Emails that contain real or perceived personal criticism feel, to the object of that criticism, materially damaging. Once such sentiments are "out there", that individual's reputation will be tarnished. Any anxiety one might have felt in the ancestral environment is multiplied by the existence of criticism in black-and-white being broadcast to any number of colleagues. This issue is exacerbated by the fact that email is stripped of the social cues available to face-to-face or phone conversation, be it facial expression, physical gestures or tone of voice. As a result, slights may be perceived rather than real. Either way, there is a desire to "set the record straight" by replying to everybody on the distribution with a differing account of facts. This can quickly escalate into a flourishing chain of emails that will not only soak up time and energy but could also damage working relationships.

So if the hunger for novelty and gossip that drives us to check incessantly for new messages, what about our proactive rather than merely reactive activity? What is it that drives us not just to reply to almost every message within seconds but to send yet more of our own? And why do people in airport executive lounges feel the need to initiate ostentatiously important phone calls? At this point, we need to take a look at another natural human urge – the quest for high status and its role in our use of technology.

CHAPTER FOUR

Status Indicators –
The Death of Hierarchy and
the Birth of Hyperactivity

"I'm going to have my lunch now.
You may go and have your dinner."

You do not need to be too close to retirement in the first decade of the twenty-first century to remember a working environment in which the organisation was much more clearly stratified. This manifested itself in any number of ways, but for some reason seemed most evident around meal times, which once were even named differently as a function of one's class.

Office life has moved a long way from mid–1960s Morgan Grenfell as related by Dominic Hobson in *The Pride of Lucifer*:

"An anecdote is still told of Lord Harcourt addressing a clerk called Cockersell..:"Cockersell, I'm going to have my lunch now. You may go and have your dinner."[xxx]

A further example I recently came across was from a friend who worked for a telecommunications equipment manufacturer which, as recently as the 1980s, felt the need to have *five* separate dining facilities – all on one site - for its 3000 employees; these comprised separate ones for rank-and-file employees, managers, scientists, directors and so on. Not only have we largely lost the habit of distinguishing between social classes by what name they give to their meals, we have seemingly lost lunch altogether.

In addition to class and dining facilities, there used to be a number of other examples of very tangible evidence of one's status; the building that I worked in with the typing-pool box also had a lift that only went to the top two floors so that the directors would not have to journey up to their offices with junior employees.

Offices and their location were an important indicator of a manager's position in the hierarchy. My own employer as recently as the late 1990s housed senior managers in double offices with their dedicated secretaries controlling access via an adjoining door. The external door between the manager's office and the corridor was locked shut. Managers of a certain grade had a bar in their office, replenished with alcoholic beverages by a lady with a trolley.

The vogue in more recent years has been to do away with some of the trappings of office. Dedicated secretaries are scarcer for middle-ranking managers since advances in technology have made them, in theory, self-sufficient in managing their communication and diaries. The physical lack of accessibility of individual offices has been reversed by the trend towards open plan offices in a drive to make senior managers more approachable, to increase organisational flexibility and to speed up decision-making.

There have undoubtedly been positive elements to the trend away from the traditional trappings of office but there has, in my view, been an unintended consequence – it has deprived the senior manager of outward signs of status, causing him or her to latch on to a surrogate: activity. One of the critical unconscious shifts in managerial behavior in the last 20 years has been to equate activity with status. This loss of physical manifestations of status has coincided with advances in communications technology that have supported the adoption of activity as a substitute. While it was previously possible to work hard and energetically in pursuit of one's objectives, prior to the information technology revolution, there were practical limits on working long hours.

The yearning for high social status is a crucial driver in human behaviour and something to be conscious of in efforts to be a better and more effective boss. Robert Wright in *The Moral Animal* writes of "the deeply human hunger for status and the seemingly universal presence of hierarchy."

Status as a concept is not limited to humans, nor even

to primates. In the 1920s, Norwegian biologist Thorlief Schjelderup-Ebbe observed a group of hens thrown together and then given some food. After an initial bout of anarchy and conflict, a clear linear hierarchy became apparent in which one hen was superior to the next, which was in turn superior to the next. In the case of a dispute over food, the higher status hen would peck the other, which would quickly yield. Schjelderup-Ebbe called this process the 'pecking order'.

Among primates – other than humans – many of the physical status signals are recognisable. As Wright puts it:

"Dominant male chimps – and dominant primates generally – strut proudly and expansively. And after two chimpanzees fight over status, the loser crouches abjectly. This sort of bowing is thereafter repeated to peacefully express submission."

If this description seems recognisable in humans in certain circumstances (such as a footballer's display after scoring a goal or missing a penalty), that is because there is indeed a biological basis for status–driven behaviour. In a civilised human society, physical battles are generally sublimated and status now gets played out to a broader audience with the help of material possessions.

In a work environment, with the withdrawal of many physical emblems of status such as prestigious office, secretary and car, one substitute measure can be your importance to the organisation as evidenced by how much you are in demand. This need to demonstrate high status is another contributing factor towards the "addiction" to the use of mobile phones and BlackBerrys. If you are truly important, it follows that people will be trying to get hold of you, wherever you are. This, in addition to the thirst for gossip, is part of the reason for constantly checking BlackBerrys for emails. So if you are contactable via mobile phone and BlackBerry, what does it say about you if you are sitting quietly in public with neither device making a noise? This is why airport business lounges and trains are full to overflowing with people initiating ostentatiously important and urgent calls ("Hi Gerry, I just wanted to let you know we had a great meeting at...").

Hence, one of the "benefits" of ubiquitous communications technology is that managers and leaders can reinforce their own sense of self-importance if they are not already overwhelmed by the volume of inbound messages; they can also *initiate* outbound messages regardless of time and almost regardless of location. Now that technology supports working around the clock, managers can signal their importance and their dedication to their bosses by emailing in the dark hours of the early morning, across the weekend or from their sun-lounger on a Caribbean beach.

Thus, the cause of this behavioural change is not the

technology itself but its role as an indicator of high status. This was evident as long ago as 1987 in Oliver Stone's *Wall Street*, where Gordon Gekko, Michael Douglas's character, stalked a takeover target with a brick-sized mobile phone while walking on the beach. It was no longer necessary to dictate a memo to a secretary to get something moving – now you could be on the beach, barking into a phone. Twenty years ago, the scarcity and expense of mobile phones was such that merely possessing one was an indicator of high status; now of course, the technology is ubiquitous. Once mobile devices became commonplace, enforcing an impression of high status became, and remains, principally achieved through the call itself – hence the cliché of the City financier shouting buy/sell instructions. As important as the call was the style in which it is made – what Gordon Gekko was doing was ushering in the Age of Aggression.

CHAPTER FIVE

"Lunch is for Wimps"
– The Rise Of Aggression

It was Gordon Gekko that famously dismissed the mid-day meal that only 20 years earlier had served as a means of class distinction in blue-blooded British banks. The year it was released was the year I left university and began work in a US-style strategy consulting boutique. The City – at least ahead of the October 1987 crash – was experiencing heady growth following the Big Bang a few years earlier, and American work practices were rapidly taking hold.

The origins of the trend towards aggression in the workplace as an indicator of status is clearly evident in accounts of the finance sector from the period. John Gutfreund of Salamon Brothers in the 1980s famously said that, in order to succeed on Salamon's trading floor a person had to wake up each morning "ready to bite the ass off a bear".[xxxi] As an illustration of how that sentiment appears to have taken hold, American hedge fund mogul Daniel Loeb had his withering email to a prospective

European recruit published in the newspapers in 2005; in it he wrote: "We are an aggressive performance oriented fund looking for blood thirsty competitive individuals who show initiative and drive to make outstanding investments".[xxxii]

I see this as something principally North American in origin and a distortion of the traditional Protestant work-ethic in the face of enormous financial incentives originating in the banking sector. The best description I have found of the original Protestant ethic can be found in Robert Jackall's 1988 book *Moral Mazes: The World of Corporate Managers*:

"A grasp of the moral significance of work in business today begins, in fact, with an understanding of the original Protestant ethic, Max Weber's term to describe the comprehensive worldview of the rising middle class that spearheaded the emergence of capitalism. The term Protestant ethic refers to the set of beliefs and, more particularly, to the set of binding social rules that counselled "secular ascetism" – the methodical, rational subjection of human impulse and desire to do God's will through "restless, continuous, systematic work in a worldly calling."[xxxiii]

This sentiment was by no means unique to the United States. Samuel Smiles published *Self Help* 150 years ago, which is replete with examples of famous British inventors that have achieved greatness through remorseless toil and often in spite of early hardships. In the United States, this ethic formed a powerful combination with the American Dream, which holds that anybody can aim for and reach the top if they simply work at it, something celebrated in the 2007 film *The Pursuit of Happyness*.

Real-life examples of what an individual could achieve in the high-stakes world of finance are well documented. Among the most memorable is Michael Lewis's portrayal of Lewie Ranieri in Liar's Poker, the classic memoir of life on Wall Street at Salomon Brothers in the mid-1980s. Ranieri began as a student working nights in the mail-room in 1968 earning $70 a week; he dropped out of college when he was made supervisor of the day-shift. He progressed to the clerical back office and then became a utility bond trader in 1974. By the mid-1980s, he was earning between two and five million dollars a year and reportedly still owned only four work suits, all of them polyester. It is hard to imagine quite the same thing happening in Europe.

When fused with the Protestant work-ethic, the result is a culture in which it is accepted that very hard work is part of getting ahead, something that did not take hold in the same way in more socially stratified Britain, in spite of Smiles's best efforts. The explicitly religious context has been lost, however; just as rewards have escalated, so has the work-rate. No longer merely restless and continuous it is now aggressive and bloodthirsty. At times, the aggressive macho posturing of the successful businessman could make one forgiven for thinking that the clock has been turned back to the ancestral environment. Michael Lewis indicated this memorably in "Liar's Poker" by noting that there was no higher accolade on the trading floor than to be called a 'Big Swinging Dick'.

Another trend in business life that provides a stage for aggressive work-rates is that of globalisation, requiring heads of international businesses to succumb to heavy travelling schedules. For some, this can be an opportunity to display a macho appetite for remorseless journeying. A "ball-breaking" travel schedule is one example of activity dependent on relatively low technology. Charles Peattie and Russell Taylor, the creators of the Alex cartoons, found their initial inspiration for Cyrus – Alex's American boss – in a conversation overheard in a London restaurant where a senior American banker boasted of having done so much air travel over the previous 12 months that he had spent only 92 nights in a proper bed.

Cyrus provides an amusing fictional illustration of a cultural US–UK divide which appears to be diminishing. Cyrus notoriously achieved a poor time in the London Marathon as he could not resist the temptation to pop into the office for a couple of hours' work. The punishing work schedule is by no means limited to the finance sector. In his memoirs, former British ambassador to the US, Sir Christopher Meyer, lamented the early departures of

American guests from social engagements on the pretext that they were so important that they had to be at their desks for six the following morning.[xxxiv]

In James B. Stewart's *DisneyWar*, a forensic account of the internal strife in Disney, Michael Eisner claims to have taken only one week off in a 28 year career in the entertainment industry. Along with other senior executives, he introduced a culture of extraordinarily long hours:

'[Jeffrey] Katzenberg's work schedule was legendary. After a few hours of sleep, he routinely arrived at the office at 5.00a.m., which tended to overshadow the fact that Eisner and [Frank] Wells worked almost as hard, often seven days a week, and expected the same of everyone else. Sometimes Wells nodded off from exhaustion, only to awake the minute someone stopped speaking. "Keep going, tell me more..." he'd say impatiently.'[xxxv]

Tragically, Wells died in 1994 in a helicopter crash during a skiing trip. At his funeral, Eisner offered these words from the podium:

'"Sleep was Frank's enemy. Frank thought that it kept him from performing flat out one hundred percent of the time. There was always one more meeting he wanted to have. Sleep, he thought, kept him from getting things done. He fought it constantly, but sleep, Frank's enemy, finally won."'

It was not always thus at Disney where, before Eisner's arrival, senior executives and producers were said to "play cards every day after lunch in a small room off the executive dining room". A newly recruited executive that insisted working evenings and weekends sparked a security investigation.

Stereotyping and business banter suggest an international spectrum ranging from work-obsessed US in the West and a more leisurely approach to work in Continental Europe in the East; the UK, naturally, lies somewhere in the middle. Referring again to Daniel Loeb's email to a prospective European recruit (for an entertaining read, see the email exchange in full in the Appendix):

"We find most brits are bit set in their ways and prefer to knock back a pint at the pub and go shooting on weekends rather than work hard. Lifestyle choices are important and knowing one's limitations with respect to dealing in a competitive environment is too. That is Lesson 1 at my shop."

Perhaps equally revealing of British attitudes to Continental European workers is a spoof news report that circulated via email around the time of the Societé General fraud perpetrated by rogue trader Jerome Kerviel:

FRIENDS of rogue trader Jerome Kerviel last night

blamed his $7 billion losses on unbearable levels of stress brought on by a punishing 30 hour week. Kerviel hid his November losses in a batch of wonderfully fresh croissant. Kerviel was known to start work as early as nine in the morning and still be at his desk at five or even five-thirty, often with just an hour and a half for lunch. One colleague said:"He was, how you say, un workaholique. I have a family and a mistress so I would leave the office at around 2pm at the latest, if I wasn't on strike.

"But Jerome was tied to that desk. One day I came back to the office at 3pm because I had forgotten my stupid little hat and there he was, fast asleep on the photocopier.

"At first I assumed he had been having sex with it, but then I remembered he had been working for almost six hours."

As the losses mounted, Kerviel tried to conceal his bad trades by covering them with an intense red wine sauce, later switching to delicate pastry horns.

At one point he managed to dispose of dozens of transactions by hiding them inside vol-au-vent cases and staging a fake reception. Last night a spokesman for Sócíété Générálé denied that Kerviel was over worked, insisting he lost the money after betting that the French were about to stop being rude, lazy, arrogant bastards.[xxxvi]

While such banter is mostly a source of international entertainment, there remains more than a ring of truth to it. There is little coherent research on international comparisons, but my experience and that of friends and colleagues suggest a different attitude does indeed prevail in Continental Europe. A friend recently observed to me that during a period in which he worked in Norway in the oil industry, few people worked excessive hours since this was regarded as a sign that you were unable to stay on top of your job.

There is some support for this view in the numbers published by the Organisation for Economic Co-operation and Development (OECD).

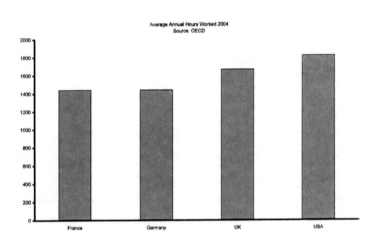

Average Annual Hours Worked 2004
Source: OECD

While the numbers are aggregated across the workforce as a whole rather than focusing on managers and leaders, figures from the OECD Employment Outlook published in 2005 suggest that there may be some truth in the stereotypes; the UK work-rate is significantly higher than that of France and Germany yet lower than that of the US.

Thus, alongside the availability of new technology and the death of hierarchy, we have the third driver which is the evolution, initially in the US, of the Protestant work ethic into a culture of aggression and extreme work practices. So when you combine the status-driven need to appear busy and aggressive with the desire to stay abreast of corporate gossip, there arises a self-fuelling upward spiral of communication. Activity is the new status.

While a return to playing cards in the afternoon may be neither desirable nor practicable, what can be done to reverse the trend towards hyperactivity? Let us begin with email and the technology that supports it. As I have argued, it is not the technology itself that drives behaviour but a number of other aspects of human psychology. Since so many of us are overwhelmed by the volume of email communication, let us begin with practical tools with which this can be addressed.

CHAPTER SIX

Taming the Technology Beast

"One of the symptoms of an approaching nervous breakdown is the belief that one's work is terribly important."
Bertrand Russell (1872 – 1970)

Amid all the complaining about email and BlackBerrys, it is sometimes easy to forget that these are tools and ultimately we, as owners and operators, control them. In trying to ease some of the problems that we associate with information technology, our solutions tend to fall into one of two categories. On the one hand, we try a draconian approach and attempt to remove the technology altogether, e.g. partially or totally. The other stance is to look for yet more technical innovations that can ease the problem.

It is a natural reaction to blame the tool and attempt to get rid of it altogether. John Cauldwell famously banned email for a period in his mobile phone business, but it proved unsustainable as all the good aspects of communication were cut out along with the bad. Some businesses have attempted email free days. Deloittes in London introduced "email-free Wednesdays" in which staff members were encouraged to avoid sending emails on Wednesdays. Inevitably, this proved impractical although Deloittes claimed partial success. "Although the actual email free day is not an email free day any more," said Mary Hensher, partner, in a BBC interview, "the actual amount of internal email circulating has dropped because people are more conscious of what they are sending."

This illustrates the futility of simply attempting to stop the problem with a Canute-like approach which, in the example of Deloittes, fell away with the "email free day" being quietly dropped. Some organisations are advised to allocate a period of the day – such as 8 until 10 each morning – to be email free. As with email free days, this can frustrate effective use of the tool by people who may be out of the office travelling and then find that their return coincides with an email free period.

As for simply banning tools altogether, I would never dream of getting rid of email or my BlackBerry under any circumstance as they give me so much flexibility and help me work fewer hours. Compare checking your email briefly on your BlackBerry with the effort of switching on a PC and logging on remotely.

Similarly, I have heard others recommend a "Zen" approach to email which involves sustaining a totally empty in-box or ditching email altogether. Leo Babauta, creator of the Zenhabits blog[xxxvii], announced in July 2009 that he was dropping email. He now uses other channels for communication with readers such as social networking service Twitter and the comments function on his blog. This approach is less achievable in a business environment where email remains, if used correctly, a powerful business tool.

The other approach of taking on more technological solutions is popular since technology vendors have an incentive to promote their products. Our collective instinct is to see any problem or issue as a question to which technology can provide the answer. There are some email plug-ins that certainly *do* make managing email easier, particularly where they include enhanced search facilities that save the laborious searches through folders of archived messages and attachments. It can also be helpful to have email connected to other channels such as social networking feeds. However, as a general principle, I do not take a technological approach when the means to reverse the vicious cycle lie not with additional external technologies, but rather, within our own minds.

What we have seen in earlier chapters is that this is not about the technology at all but rather the psychology of the human animal. Our natural instinct is to check email to see what is happening to our positioning in the world – we have a well-established need to stay on top of the gossip; in a business environment where traditional trappings of status have evaporated, we feel the need to be seen as busy and in demand; and, of course, we want to get things done quickly.

In order to reverse the trend towards high levels of inefficient activity at work, we need to reverse some of these psychological processes. If the right state of mind can be established, particularly among the organisation's leadership, technological symptoms of inefficient hyperactivity – such as crippling levels of email – can be removed.

Email

Let us take email to start with and how a simple code with eleven principles can change an organisation's relationship with it. In addition to the impact of high volumes of email, there are the negative effects of what one sufferer described to me pejoratively as an "email culture" in his company. This is the pernicious habit of hiding behind email for communication of bad or difficult news; of covering one's backside by copying someone in a long thread which the sender perceives has ticked the box of informing the recipient in some way; of throwing an action over the wall marked with a red flag. In this sort of culture, the obligation is on the recipient to wade through a complex thread to find the nugget of important information. A "red flag" email is an example of responsibility being transferred from the sender to the recipient with a deadline and a categorisation of urgency that has not been agreed. These behaviours contribute to stress and irritation and drive up the level of anxiety to the point that people feel the need to be tied continually to their in-boxes. They drive up email volumes as people feel compelled to reply widely to resist actions and deadlines that have not been agreed. They also feel loss of control when red flags, deadlines and items on their task bar are imposed by other people.

There are two dimensions to the effective use of email: firstly, the cultural environment and secondly, the habits and practice of the individual. While the latter is under one's direct control, it is the organisational climate that will drive the experience for most people, so let us begin with that.

One corporate approach is to control the technology from the centre. The initiative that appears to be most common and which does *not* contribute to the reduction of email-related stress is to reduce the maximum size of email folders. In one company I worked, the IP-based phone system was linked to the email in-box so, when your in-box was full, your voicemail stopped working also. Working life felt like an unending process of trying to bale out a leaking boat.

Christina Cavanagh in her research into email at the University of Toronto found as follows:

"What was found lacking was evidence that organizations were taking a proactive role in helping their employees deal with email management. Most initiatives were undertaken by individuals on an ad hoc basis. The only initiative that did come from some organizations was restricting mailbox size so that end users were forced to archive or delete items in order to regain full use of their in-boxes. While this is a legitimate IT solution to conserve server storage capacity, it needs to be combined with measures in organizations to reduce volumes at the source. Most respondents found that restricting in-box size only served to create greater stress – they were usually forced to interrupt their work routines just to clear out their in-boxes."[xxxviii]

I would liken this approach to finding a man in a water-filled chamber standing on a stool to keep his head above water – and then taking away the stool. Other approaches include disabling the "Reply to All" function, something that the CIO of Nielsen Media Research reportedly resorted to. Used correctly, this function is a useful time-saver and I would argue that in order to stop its misuse, it is the behaviour that needs to be addressed rather than the technology.

There is much more that an organisation should and can do. So, looking at a more positive behavioural approach to the issue, you as leader should be in a position to implement an email policy at least among the people that work for you. Ideally, if employee feedback is telling you that the volume of email communication is a significant problem, you should be able to get support for a company-wide initiative.

In one of my corporate roles, I was able to persuade my then boss to implement a "code" for email use across the several hundred people working in his directorate. A staff conference gave us an opportunity to present it to the entire team in one session and the impact was very positive.

As a general principle, an organisation's leadership must be seen to lead by example. This is likely to involve a break with existing practice and may be personally difficult for some. It needs enforcing with some vigour by the organisation's leadership and senior management.

If the introduction of a new "code" is not taken seriously, then it will go the way of countless other initiatives as enthusiasm dissipates and people return to their old ways. I recently spoke to someone who experienced a company-wide directive on the use of email at the large consultancy she worked for; this was ignored after what she described as "a couple of weeks of luke-warm compliance". Furthermore, if the underlying psychological cultural issues are not addressed, then senior managers will smile wryly at the guidelines and continue the "macho" approach of emailing at all hours. Senior managers need to lead from the front and all staff must actively coach and feed back to their peers when codes are violated.

For the code to become effective, violation needs to

become socially unacceptable. After all, the growing understanding of the impact of stress and long-hours makes it very clear that not addressing the issue of information overload via email can contribute directly and indirectly to drivers of ill-health such as stress and poor sleep. The health threats of passive smoking are universally accepted to the point that, in the UK, it is now unthinkable for someone to light a cigarette in the office – anyone doing so would bring instant opprobrium upon themselves. *Inappropriate use of email needs to be treated by colleagues as if someone has just lit a cigarette in the office.*

Here are the components of the organisational email code:

1) We will not use email as our first resort for internal communication
Let us begin with what email is really good for. In the days of the internal memo, routine administrative information had to be distributed to everyone on paper. This could cover anything from a new fire drill procedure or announcing the arrival of a new team member. These non-urgent, broadcasts of information are perfect for email. If you have received something significant from an external customer or partner, forwarding that email to relevant colleagues is an enormously efficient way of communicating that information directly. Among teams distributed across many locations, email has an important role as a communications device. And yet, it is easy to overlook the

importance of direct personal contact in getting work done. This is true of relationships with external customers but equally true of relationships within teams. As someone that used to work for me often said, "People do business".

When employees look at their over-flowing email in-boxes, it is remarkable how much of that volume is internal and of that, how much is from colleagues in the same physical office. As an exercise, look at how many emails have come from people seated at desks within your field of vision. While the latest technology allows people to work in an increasingly solitary way, effective team-working requires frequent personal contact. We will come to the importance of this later, but it is impossible to over-estimate the importance of people engaging directly as much as possible.

So as a point of principle, if it is possible to talk face-to-face with a colleague instead of sending an email, then that should be the means of communication. If that individual is not available, then the next best option is to pick up the phone. Email should be the last resort.

One of the reasons that face-to-face communication is preferred, particularly for anything sensitive or personal, is that it enables participants to draw on the non-verbal components of a conversation that research tells us make up such an important part of it. The exact proportion of communication made up by such factors as posture, language, facial gestures and tone of voice is disputed;

nevertheless, as social animals we are enormously dependent on them in order to establish personal relationships.

We are often not conscious of the importance of these aspects of personal contact and so when, in email, we look solely at the written word, it is easy to misinterpret the intent of the sender. An extreme example of this was covered in the press in 2009. Vicki Walker, an accountant at New Zealand healthcare provider ProCare Health, had endured a long struggle with staff failing to fill out their expense forms correctly, something that resulted in delays in payment. To ensure that her colleagues got their money as quickly as possible, she sent an email with an exhortation in blue capitals:

"TO ENSURE YOUR STAFF CLAIM IS PROCESSED AND PAID, PLEASE DO FOLLOW THE BELOW CHECK LIST."

Mrs Walker was sacked after colleagues complained that her email was too "shouty". This was in spite of the fact that she was attempting to help them. She was ultimately compensated for unfair dismissal at an employment tribunal. The case illustrates the extent to which email can be misinterpreted. Many guides exist to "netiquette" – the art of crafting email messages with the correct etiquette – and the issue is well-covered in David Shipley and Will Schwalbe's excellent book on email *Send*.[xxxix]

I agree with the importance of getting the tone of email right, but would not place this above the importance of using face-to-face communication wherever possible.

An additional reason that email communication is often the preferred form of communication is that it provides a documented trail of what has been said; this is distinct from a verbal communication which may later be forgotten or disputed. There are two problems with this principle: firstly, it is a "backside covering" impulse which suggests a trust problem between sender and receiver; secondly, it is unilateral and does not reflect any agreement between the two parties, possibly leading to an extended negotiation – via email. As such, it is an example of a negative email culture that reflects a context of poor personal relationships. In this situation, there is all the more need to meet face-to-face in order to improve the relationship. Once an agreement has been reached, this can by all means be documented in a brief email with a summary of the points agreed. If the relationship is right, the message can be archived and should not need to be referred to again.

2) We will not email out of hours except in exceptional circumstances
In Chapter 1 I explained how the Japanese concept of *karoshi* revolves around working excessively long hours. We have seen how email makes this easier than ever, so the principle of not emailing out of hours is an important one. I have spoken to people working for a Group Finance

Director of a major British public company who were accustomed to coming into work and seeing emails from him that had been sent as early as five-thirty in the morning. Others in his peer group frequently sent emails late into the night and across the weekend. The result is a "virtual presenteeism" that means even managers too junior to be equipped with BlackBerrys feel obliged to log in to their email on a Sunday evening to keep up to date with the chatter. While the temptation with BlackBerrys is to scan them continuously for recent communication, they are most powerful as a tool when the 'off' button is used for evenings and weekends.

If an organisation's leadership explicitly enforces a culture of respecting employees' time outside working hours, the spiralling threads of emails across evenings and weekends will diminish. Of course, it remains important for people to remain contactable in emergencies, but there are ways to do that which do not intrude on personal time.

Of course, the definition of an emergency is a subjective one. If in doubt as to whether one needs to interrupt someone's weekend, I would always ask: What is the worst that will happen if we leave this until Monday? If I do need to be contacted, my personal preference is to be contactable by text message in the evenings, weekends and during holidays. I divert my phone to voicemail during evenings and weekends and, if a message is left, I receive a text message. When on holiday, I change my voicemail message to refer enquiries to a team member with delegated authority. That person can get hold of me via SMS if needed. This principle has always worked for me, including when running a public company. If, having been alerted to something urgent, I am then sent an email with further information, then that strikes me as a good use of the technology. In order to operate according to this principle, you will need to have a mobile phone that is not your BlackBerry.

3) We will not use email for negative feedback or "flaming"

We shall come also to the role of negative feedback which, managed constructively, is an important tool. However, email is a poor medium through which to communicate negative issues. For one thing, its speed and ease of use mean that it is all too easy to bash out an indignant message that the sender will regret once they have had a chance to cool down. Secondly, as we have already observed, it lacks the social cues of face-to-face communication. What was intended as a mild rebuke or an ironic bit of banter can be interpreted as an outright insult by the recipient. Thirdly, by copying others in on the email, the sender is slighting a colleague in full view of peers. This inevitably stimulates a self-justifying response, also copied to all. As well as being a distraction for all on the receiving end of the email, this form of communication is prone to escalation as some of the other recipients feel the need to clear the air also.

It is easier to send an email to someone containing negative segments than to confront them face-to-face. But it is far better to take a grievance directly to the person concerned than to send an email. Failing that, a phone call is still infinitely better than an email.

For those on the receiving end of a negative email, the temptation to send an equally vitriolic "reply-to-all" missive in the other direction should be resisted. If a reply is needed at all, it should be along the lines of:

"Thank you for your message. As you might expect, I cannot accept what you say but do not think it makes sense to continue the dialogue over email. I will make contact with you off-line."

This can be copied to everyone on the original email without fear of escalation, but at the same time affirming your rejection of its sentiments.

4) We will not use email for complex discussions

When I had the opportunity to introduce my email code to my then boss's 1500-strong organisation, I brandished a print-out of an email debate on a particularly complex eclectic bit of future regulation that had been copied to me and a few others in the team. It had been copied to me on every instalment as each new contribution was made as a "reply-to-all" email. The print-out ran to fourteen pages.

Each time we receive an email in our in-box, it takes a certain amount of time and mental energy even to determine that it ought to be deleted. Debates about complex issues are difficult to read on email as you need to start from bottom-up to understand the 'thread' of the conversation. It is a poor medium for debate as people find themselves re-reading previous messages with each new instalment to reacquaint themselves with the issues.

A far better approach is to pull together a small group of relevant people and aim to tackle the issue in one meeting or conference call. If an email 'thread' looks as if it is mushrooming into a complex debate, send a message to all on the copy list informing them that the issue will be managed "off-line" and how.

5) We will not "red-flag" email as urgent

In my view, there is no such thing as an urgent email. If something is genuinely time-critical and somebody is required to do something, then at the very least a phone call is warranted. Microsoft Outlook does have some inventive features; among these is the ability to "flag" an email as urgent with a deadline, beyond which a red flag will actually appear on screen.

There are a number of problems with this. Firstly, the degree of urgency is subjective and something that is urgent in the mind of the sender may not be so urgent for the recipient. Secondly, the red flag is distracting and contributes to the frenzied whirl of messages that increases stress and reduces effectiveness. Thirdly, the use of such a feature implies a) the absolution in the sender of any responsibility to see the issue through, and b) an assumption that the recipient is looking at their email. Once the use of red flags takes hold, everybody feels under pressure to check emails frequently in case there is anything urgent that needs them to take care of.

A particularly pernicious feature of the red flag option is the ability of the sender to create for the recipient a reminder and a presence on the taskbar. This should be in the exclusive control of the recipient, otherwise there is the risk that the resulting loss of control will increase stress. This is one feature of Microsoft Outlook that I recommend is disabled at the server level if possible.

6) We will extract salient information when forwarding long threads
Another practice that people tell me frustrates them is that of forwarding long emails, which put the burden on the recipient to figure out which bit of information is important. If, as is likely, they miss it and find out at some point when the information would have been of use, it is of no help to be told: "It's there – in the thread." Use email positively and proactively: either delete the irrelevant parts of the thread or cut-and-paste the part your recipient needs to see. Make life a little easier for people and they may do the same for you.

These six points need to be observed throughout an organisation if they are to have an impact. The leadership bears the greatest responsibility of all for their enforcement. There are general themes across these points that reflect the culture of an organisation and the spirit in which email is used. If everyone observes them, then email can return to being a tool rather than an external force that appears to reduce everybody's effectiveness.

Once the code is adopted and working effectively, use of email can be made more efficient still with some tips for individuals to follow. I emphasise that these tips will not help in an organisational environment in which people are still receiving several hundred emails a day, nor one in which it is assumed that they are constantly checking new messages. Once the organisational code has been adopted, these tips for the individual should offer further help:

1) Tackle e-mail in concentrated bouts

It is quite possible for people in corporate environments to spend their whole working day tinkering with their email in-box. Christina Cavanagh of the University of Toronto estimates that as much as 12 per cent of a company's payroll is spent on ineffective use of email. While ploughing through the in-box may feel like a full day's work to the individual, it is unlikely to have helped with objectives or moved the company forward in any way. Email is best tackled in short bursts where incoming messages can be dealt with swiftly. Set up time in which to do this, such as a half-hour to an hour first thing in the morning.

Focusing on email in this way will help avoid unproductive but time-consuming email flitting. When overwhelmed with large volumes of messages, this can take the form of opening a previously opened message to remind yourself of the contents and then closing it again. It is common practice to mark a read email as unread as a reminder that you need to deal with it. Approaching email in this way as a continuous task amidst other activities is hugely inefficient. It is far better to tackle the in-box in a determined and focused way for a sustained period each day.

The key word here is 'tackle'. This means acting decisively on messages so that they can be deleted or archived. If a reply is required, that can be done directly. If some other action is required, such as reading an attachment, that can be done later. If you feel the message may be needed at some point in the future, then store it in a folder or create one for it. The important thing is to clear messages as effectively as possible.

I have come across some email coaches that advocate a "one-touch" policy: this suggests that once you open an email, you deal with it at once. According to this principle, you either delete it, archive it or forward it. I think this approach brings with it the risk of firing from the hip –

sometimes, an email can be closed down at once but at other times it will need a considered response or will require you to do something offline. In this case, the email remains in your in-box as something that needs to be dealt with. Forwarding or replying quickly for the sake of removing may unwittingly result in yet more email, particularly if part of the message has been mis-read or misunderstood.

I recently came across a company of accountants that instigated an email-free period from eight to ten each morning that each employee was told they had to adhere to. As covered earlier when we looked at company-wide initiatives, I find this approach something of a blunt instrument and unhelpful – not least because eight in the morning is my preferred time for tackling email in a concentrated bout. I prefer to leave it to the individual to choose when they tackle email, as company-wide directives will inevitably cause inconvenience not least because there will be occasions when the email-free period will sometimes coincide with the only period people have in the office between external meetings.

2) Be ruthless with deletion and filing

If in doubt, delete. Be rigorous in deleting emails where the content is repeated in replies. Set up as many folders as needed in which to store emails that you prefer not to delete. There is nothing wrong in hoarding emails, but ensure that the in-box is as empty as possible. Unsubscribe to any newsletters or automated messages that are not delivering value to you. Use Outlook's "rules" capability to have messages that you plan to read but which are not time-critical – such as a bulletin – sent straight to a folder without hitting the in-box.

Using folders is an important part of email management. If you are worried about being unable to find the message in the future, use a plug-in to your email that includes a search engine.

3) Make sure you can see the bottom of your in-box

This may sound mundane but it has an enormous impact. Being able to see the bottom of the in-box on one screen – this generally means having no more than about *thirty* emails in there at some point each day – has a greater psychological impact than you might think. There is something forbidding and depressing about a list that scrolls down, beyond your field of vision, with any number of messages requiring action. In addition to the depressing feeling that comes with it, a large in-box inevitably results in messages being forgotten and not replied to. The consequence of this is that actions will go uncompleted and colleagues, customers or suppliers will feel put out if their messages are not acknowledged. If, like an overweight man that has not seen his toes in years, you are not familiar with the feeling, get your in-box down to this level and feel how liberating it is. Knowing that you have your in-box under control will free you to get on with other activities with a lighter heart. Naturally, it will fill up again, particularly if you are out of the office, but if you keep up the discipline, it will usually take little more than a small burst of activity to get it down again.

A similar approach is the "In-box Zero" strategy first recommended by Merlin Mann. This approach is different insofar as it recommends taking all actions out of your in-box and moving them either to a folder marked "Action" or migrating them to the task functionality of Microsoft Outlook. Some will tell you that leaving emails that require action in your in-box creates a *de facto* action list and this is the path to disaster. I can see nothing wrong with having a small (i.e. fewer than thirty) emails in your in-box that you know have to be dealt with. I have always used this strategy successfully and take the view that moving them to another folder is akin to shuffling the deckchairs on the Titanic. Because they *are* in another folder, it then becomes easy to forget about them and easier still for them to accumulate to the point where they fill more than one screen. So all that has been achieved is the movement of the overflowing in-box to a folder.

The most important point here is the development of the habit of approaching the in-box with discipline and vigour for sustained periods but only once or twice a day, dealing with your in-box as quickly and effectively as possible.

4) Turn off all email alerts

We know that being inundated with several messages at once via different communications channels reduces effectiveness. The work by psychologist Glenn Wilson suggested that the impact of frequent interruptions on the IQ was a reduction of ten points.

The impact of new emails is exacerbated by the ability to have Microsoft Outlook indicate the arrival of a new email with as many of four types of alert. By simultaneously using sound and visual cues, these alerts have a detrimental impact on the brain's processing power – it's almost as if they were designed to slow down our cognitive ability.

The answer is simple. Turn off all indicators of new email.

5) Exit email completely when focusing on other work

When you are doing something that requires focus and sustained effort such as working on a document or presentation, exit your email altogether. Remember that there is no such thing as an urgent email. If somebody needs your help urgently, let them call you. Your email can wait until you are able to give it your full attention.

Blackberry

BlackBerrys, while being very useful when used properly, also enable us to take all of the negative, disruptive aspects of email and carry them around with us all day. They are designed to fuel the anxiety that the latest email just might be something important and which you do not want to miss out on. The buzz that alerts you at night on the bedside table or the flashing light that turns from red to green play right into the psychological anxieties surrounding status and gossip. However, the impact is felt not only by us as individuals seated at our desks – it can be felt by colleagues, friends and family in meetings, social engagements and at home.

Dr Wilson's study at King's College, London also found his subjects checking messages in meetings in spite of nine out of ten believing that it was rude to do so. Even while acknowledging the rudeness of this practice, a third nonetheless felt that this had become "acceptable and seen as a sign of diligence and efficiency". Our psychological thirst to be on top of the gossip has superseded any aversion we might have had to being perceived as rude; we have become desensitized to the erosion of common courtesies.

It is not uncommon in corporate meeting rooms to find attendees using their BlackBerrys even while presentations are being given. I have frequently known colleagues emailing each other across a meeting room table while a colleague was presenting. I once attended a meeting where the divisional Managing Director was observed looking at his BlackBerry while one of the people in his organisation was presenting a proposal for approval. With only a slight hint of irony he said when challenged, "But meetings are the only chance I get to do my emails."

What signal can it send to someone presenting to a meeting of senior managers if some or all are checking their emails on their BlackBerry? The diligence and efficiency is directed entirely upwards, i.e. the manager is fulfilling the need to respond promptly to messages from people higher up in the hierarchy. However, he is giving the message to people in the same room that his email is taking higher priority than the content of the meeting or presentation.

One of the impacts of the BlackBerry is to make status a constant issue. In a large meeting or gathering with a range of people from different levels in the hierarchy, it is natural for people to pay most attention to those at the top. In the pre-BlackBerry era, these senior managers would not be front of mind in a small meeting with more junior people. However, the BlackBerry ensures that their virtual presence is continuous making the representations of junior managers seem inconsequential.

Before looking at how to fix this, it is worth considering this issue for a moment in terms of the old-fashioned virtues of courtesy and respect. I mention these not as ends in themselves, even though I happen to believe they genuinely do make the world a better place; even the laziest, most self-interested boss needs to fall back on them to get the best out of his people. For an individual to work effectively and diligently, it is important that they believe in what they are doing and that their work is making a contribution to their company, division or team. If they are in a meeting with peers or seniors, nothing can undermine this more than the sight of the attendees glancing at their BlackBerrys beneath the table.

Some companies, reportedly including Microsoft, now insist that, for certain meetings, mobile devices are left outside the room. There really is only one rule required to implement better use of the BlackBerry: TURN IT OFF at inappropriate occasions. To my mind, these include:

- during meetings
- during social occasions
- at evenings and weekends once you are with family
- on holiday.

As mentioned earlier, you can remain contactable by having a mobile phone in addition to your BlackBerry; having your BlackBerry as your mobile phone means that you will always be tempted to glance at emails. If you operate in this way consistently and if your colleagues understand this, you will find that the BlackBerry is transformed into a powerful business tool.

Mobile Phones

I am mystified by the behaviour of people who answer

calls on their mobile only to say: "Er, actually, I'm on holiday." In spite of myself, I apologise even though I had no possible way of knowing that he or she was away. The way in which to get the best out of a mobile phone is to switch it off on all the same occasions when a BlackBerry should be switched off. If it is important to be able to receive voicemail and text messages, leave it on but divert it to voicemail.

Handling Emergencies

There are inevitably occasions when there is a genuine need for people to be contactable out of hours. My preference is to leave a mobile phone on but diverted to voicemail. This allows me to pick up SMS messages when a new message has been left. I have always found this perfectly adequate wherever I have worked. Having picked up the message, I can then either call the person back or switch on my BlackBerry and pick up relevant emails. This is an effective and non-intrusive way of being contactable. It also helps to have a mobile phone that is not your BlackBerry.

What To Do When On Holiday

One of the benefits of the latest communications technology is that it comes equipped with a number of tools and devices to make life easier. If you have successfully established for you and your organisation an environment where it is acceptable *not* to check emails and take phone calls when on holiday, this needs to be implemented effectively.

1. Emergency contact

The need for constant contact evaporates if people close to you such as direct reports, boss, secretary/PA can get hold of you if something really does need your urgent attention. I think it is entirely reasonable for contact to be made if it is really felt necessary, and there are any number of ways of enabling this in a way that is not disruptive:

- if you are staying in a hotel, let your secretary have the number so that she can leave a message
- if you do not have a secretary to act as a gatekeeper, offer to check SMS messages once a day. I have done this for the last few years and found it highly effective without being disruptive. I tend to leave my mobile phone switched off in the hotel bedroom, switching it on once every day or two just to pick up texts.

2. Voicemail

Mobile phone networks now make it easy for the consumer to change voicemail messages. "I will now be on holiday until (date). If you need urgent help, please contact (name and number of colleague)." This is a simple and effective way of ensuring that you are not plagued on holiday.

3. Email

You cannot prevent email coming in but switching on the "Out of office autoreply" feature lets everyone sending a message know that you are away. This means that they are informed not to expect a response from you until your return. Also provide the email address of a colleague that people can get hold of if they need something before your return.

If we accept that working longer hours may not only make us less effective in our work but unhappier in our lives, then there is a range of steps we can take in order to reverse the vicious circle.

Arguably the most immediate and apparent symptom of hyperactive work practices is the ballooning use of email, mobiles and BlackBerrys. But there are other symptoms of hyperactivity such as kicking off too many initiatives. Effective work practices, including the use of technology, starts with the recognition that tangible success is rarely a function of how many emails you send; it is more likely to result from doing a small number of big things – really well.

CHAPTER SEVEN

Focus

"To do two things at once is to do neither."
Publilius Syrus, 1ˢᵗ Century Roman sage

We have seen that activity has, with the erosion of traditional indicators of seniority, become an indicator of status, something exacerbated by the ubiquity of communications technology. If, having understood the psychological drivers that contribute to the trend towards hyperactivity, we take a fresh look at our working lives, it becomes possible to do away with other ineffective practices. Rather than assume that we are obliged to work as hard as possible across as broad a range of activities as we can manage, we need to examine the relationship between effort and outcome. This is where focus comes in.

In his book *The Eighty-Twenty Principle*, Richard Koch has very eloquently captured the overwhelming importance of focus and how the Pareto Principle can be applied at work and to life in general.[xl] For me, it is required reading for anyone who wants to achieve a lot without having to work themselves into the ground, so I do not plan to repeat the book's content in any length here. At its core is the long-established principle named after nineteenth century Italian economist Vilfredo Pareto, which suggests that 80 per cent of the value in any given scenario comes from 20 per cent of the effort. In the context of a business's revenue, it generally turns out to be the case that something in the order of 80 per cent comes from the top 20 per cent of customers. This has been long understood. Where Koch had an incremental impact was to extend the analogy to personal effort: 80 per cent of what you achieve will be delivered by 20 per cent of your effort. Extended to its logical conclusion, this means that once you have achieved a certain number of tasks, the impact of your continued effort falls subject to the law of diminishing returns. In an ideal world, you would simply down tools after expending the highly effective 20 per cent and take it easy. Of course, it does not work quite like that, but can the Pareto Principle apply in a modern corporate environment?

In James Stewart's history of Disney's internal strife, he acknowledges that Michael Eisner's early tenure was highly successful and accompanied by a growth in operating income of less than $300 million in 1984 to almost $800 million in 1987.

"An internal analysis commissioned by Gary Wilson to help understand the company's burgeoning profit found that nearly all of it came from just three sources: raising admission prices at the theme parks; greatly expanding the number of company-owned hotels; and distributing the animated classics on home video."

How much of this success is attributable to Eisner is questionable; nevertheless, it is a powerful illustration of how commercial success can be concentrated in such a small number of activities.

I have found it possible to take a similar approach to your own job. I once had a near-inspirational insight from one former boss with whom I had a "one-to-one" meeting early on in our relationship. It being a new financial year, one of the items for discussion at the meeting was my annual set of objectives. As was the custom at this company, and most others, I had drafted a document running to two or three pages with a series of bullet points in small type listing all the various things I would achieve over the next year. There were at least two dozen objectives listed, a number that I felt was needed to justify my position and also reflect what a highly industrious person I was.

To my surprise, my boss languidly put my document to one side and said, "If we were to fast-forward one year and look back to this point in time, what three big things could you have done that would make you reflect: 'That was a pretty good year'?"

After a bit of thought, I came up with three big-ticket, ambitious and high impact initiatives. We agreed that I should have these as my objectives. As the year progressed, I was able to pull off all three, with the support of my team.

What this experience taught me was that by focusing on a small number of big objectives, I was able to achieve some very significant things. One of them was a major product innovation that was resisted in many parts of the company but was ultimately described as a "stunning success" by our chief executive. Part of the reason that I was successful was because I was sufficiently clear-headed to tackle the many internal issues head-on. Precisely because I had not cluttered myself and my team with innumerable small issues, we were able to stay on top of the three key projects. I doubt I ever gave another thought to the smaller more marginal objectives that I had discarded; some of them will have happened in any case, but the point remains that I achieved much more through attempting less.

I have since always followed the strategy of tackling each of the two or three major objectives and giving them sustained focused effort. Taking the 80:20 principle to a further level, it is often the case that success against these objectives will pivot around one or two key events, possibly a bid or a presentation. It might be something less formal such as an otherwise casual conversation with a key influencer. Investing energy and time in these pivotal events is fundamentally important and will yield success. I have seen senior managers and leaders miss such opportunities as they have approached them from within a cloud of hyperactivity. Initiative overload arises when leaders succumb to the temptation to kick off a number of activities in the mistaken belief that doing something is always better than doing nothing. This mind-set is often in evidence in government as well as in business where large volumes of legislative initiatives are pushed through even though they are often poorly drafted and ill-considered. It is, if anything, braver to identify what action will address 80 per cent of the issue and to recognise that any additional initiative may double effort but have negligible incremental impact. There are some circumstances where the right answer to a given situation is to do nothing at all. It is brave to hold this course when others are calling for something to be done. This pressure drives us to reach for something and then do it, regardless of its merits. It is motivated by a need to reduce anxiety and fails to account for the wasteful expenditure of resources.

We have looked at the evidence that the current vogue for trying to manage large volumes of emails, phone calls and so on has a strikingly negative impact on cognitive ability. Therefore, once we have identified a small number of important things to work on, we need to focus on them in a sustained way rather than paying piecemeal attention to them in the midst of a welter of other activities. Saint Ignacius of Loyola, the first Father General of the Jesuits, would be regarded as a leadership guru if he were alive today rather than the fifteenth century; echoing Publilius Syrus, he once said: "He who does well one work at a time, does more than all."

In order to achieve focus, you need to be sufficiently disciplined not to flit between tasks. We all succumb to the temptation to look at our email when hitting a block in writing a document. As we have seen, there is no shortage of external interruptions without providing our own. So, as advised in the section on email, it is best to exit the in-box altogether when focusing on a discrete piece of work.

Urgent vs. Important

In the frenzied blur of email and multimedia messaging, it is easy to fall into the trap of regarding everything as high priority. Messages from our boss or other high-status individuals – particularly when several people are also copied in – feel as if they need to be dealt with and replied to quickly in order to demonstrate that we are responsive and "on the case". Dealing with it may involve us calling in resources from within our own organisation and so we require people in our teams to drop what they are doing and deal with this "urgent" issue.

The urgency in this sort of situation derives not from

any business imperative but from our need to demonstrate responsiveness in a culture of hyperactivity and messaging overload. Since activity has become an indicator of status, the speed and industry that we can demonstrate in responding to something should mark us out as worthy of higher status.

However, this chain reaction says nothing about the importance of any given activity to the business or the impact of doing nothing about it immediately or ever. We are often tempted to treat something as urgent merely because it is a new piece of communication. For every communication, before firing from the hip and drawing in additional resources to respond, we need to ask ourselves to what extent this task is important. Is it pivotal to the small number of key objectives that will deliver the 80 per cent of value we are working towards?

Time Management

If we are working in a frenzied, hyperactive environment, it is all too easy to attribute our failure to complete important tasks and to deliver our objectives on the lack of time. It is equally easy to look to time management as a solution to this issue. This would be a mistake.

Firstly, when we identify time – or lack of it – as the root of our problems, we are identifying an abstract notion and attaching to it a causal relationship with all of our difficulties. It is not time that is our problem; rather it is all the unproductive, inefficient and unnecessary activity with which we fill it.

I was given a graphic illustration of this when I was lucky enough to watch a group of eleven highly intelligent and ambitious MBA students perform a simple and brief outdoor team exercise in 20 minutes. In their eagerness to complete the exercise in record time, they launched straight into it under the *de facto* leadership of the group's alpha male... and performed lamentably. Having made a disaster of the first attempt, they had plenty of time and made a second one which was fractionally better. In all, they were able to make seven attempts. They were naturally disappointed when told at the end that their best time was poorer than that achieved by a group of primary school children a week earlier. The fact was that they had given themselves no time to discuss different ways of approaching the task and had only chanced upon the optimal way of completing it towards the very end when it was too late. Five minutes of planning and discussion at the outset might have secured a different outcome altogether. When the self-appointed leader was asked to reflect upon why they had performed so poorly, in spite of having had seven attempts at the task, his analysis was: "We ran out of time."

The route to effectiveness is not through managing time any differently. Instead, it is about thinking very carefully about the way in which we approach tasks so that not only do we cut out unimportant activity, but that we also think and plan hard as we approach the important activity that remains. Much inefficiency and urgent activity within organisations is the "cost of failure" resulting from not doing something correctly first time. Failure is more likely to happen in an environment of frenzied hyperactivity when the task in question is being juggled with innumerable others and when key people are hurried, stressed and operating with impaired cognitive ability and short-term memory.

The Myth of Multi-Tasking

One of the least desirable by-products of the hyperactive age of work is the belief that we can conduct multiple activities at once. At an extreme level, we risk putting the lives of others in danger such as when we drive while trying to use the phone at the same time. On other occasions, we diminish the impact of at least one of the tasks we are attempting to do. In his research, Nathan Zeldes tells of a senior technologist who acquired the latest Harry Potter novel in ebook format so that he could read it to his son at bed-time and read his emails at the same time.

To illustrate how the brain copes with multi-tasking, let us look at the research conducted at the Center for Cognitive Brain Imaging, part of the Department of Psychology at Carnegie Mellon University. A team led by

Marcel Just used MRI scanning to measure the brain activity and performance of a number of subjects while performing simultaneous tests that used different parts of the brain. On the one hand, subjects were asked questions that tested the language comprehension system by having general knowledge statements read to them and being asked to judge whether or not they were true; at the same time, they were asked to look at abstract 3D drawings that had to be mentally rotated in order to be identified – this task used the brain's visuo-spatial system which is completely independent of the part of the brain that supports language. Just's team compared speed and accuracy with separate performance of the tasks as stand-alone undertakings. What the research concluded was that while there was little decline in accuracy of the language task when comparing dual versus stand-alone tasks, there was an increase in response time of approaching 50 per cent; for the mental rotation task, both accuracy and response times were significantly poorer when performed as dual tasks. This is the first piece of research to look at dual activities in parts of the brain that do not overlap, and what the scientists conclude is that the brain has "biological mechanisms that place an upperbound limit on the amount of cortical tissue that can be activated at any given time".[xli] Without speculating on evolutionary reasons why this might be the case, it strikes me as quite sensible – from an evolutionary perspective – to have these constraints built in against over-usage. What we are doing when we multi-task – even when we use separate parts of our brain for respective activities – is invoking the brain's internal throttle which has an impact both on accuracy and speed.

I often hear it said of young people that "multi-tasking comes naturally" to them, that they are "wired differently" and that they are better skilled at working simultaneously with communication across a number of channels and devices. It is certainly the case that young people are more accustomed to this way of working – never having known anything different. Nothing can demonstrate the generation gap more starkly for someone who left university in the 1980s or earlier than watching a twenty-first century information worker in front of their computer screen; the display is a patchwork of newsfeeds, stock-trackers and even web-cams. Normal as this may seem to this generation of technology users, they are wired in precisely the same way as everybody else. The scientific evidence on the negative impact of multi-tasking on our cognitive ability is as true of young people as it is of their seniors.

Micromanagement – failing to see the wood for the trees

Micromanagement is the pejorative expression for what managers do when they fail to focus. It manifests itself firstly as very detailed involvement in the day-to-day work of subordinates; secondly, because of the ease of communication across levels of the organisation, it is also a symptom of the failure to delegate. It is, in part, a function of the mindset which regards drilling down into every last detail as an indicator of corporate machismo. I have met a number of chief executives who prided themselves in being on top of every last number of every product line, retail outlet or business plan in their organisation; while impressive as a feat of mental gymnastics, this behaviour always appears to me to correlate with a frenetic, work-obsessed lifestyle in which work continues throughout holidays and family life is relegated to a distant second priority behind the needs of the office. I once had a review of my division's profit and loss with our chief executive whose own annual revenue line was in the order of £15 billion; I remember being amazed that we spent 20 minutes discussing the accounting treatment of a £1,500 licence fee, something that had no cash impact on the business whatsoever. This meretricious and sometimes ostentatious involvement in the minutiae of a company is fuelled by the prevalence of electronic communications technology; once a chief executive regards activity as an indicator of status, involvement in microscopic aspects of the organisation is an inevitable consequence. In addition to undermining the necessary practice of delegation, the habit also undermines the individual's ability to focus on the small number of important things that may determine the fate of the organisation.

The Elimination of Activity for its Own Sake

For many, this is a fundamental change of mind-set – a transition away from an attitude towards activity that sees it as directly correlating with achievement. This means cutting out activity for its own sake.

Anybody can work long hours, email at ridiculous times of the day or night and make contact when on holiday. This activity does not in of itself make money, deliver objectives or do anything other than signal the individual's presence. It is much more demanding to ask that person what progress they have made on the two or three fundamental objectives that you have identified as being genuinely impactful.

For people in an organisation to deliver against a small number of high impact objectives, it is important to reverse the cycle of unproductive but high-energy work practices; such practices may be time-consuming and energy-sapping, but in a way they are also liberating. Rather than thinking hard about how to make tangible progress against objectives, even senior managers can fill their days just trying to tackle their email in-boxes. They are working hard – as is everybody else – but not necessarily being effective.

We shall come to the importance of delegation and the need to trust employees as far as possible. But it is the leader who sets the tone for the way in which people work. Activity for its own sake achieves little or nothing; it can, at high levels, be destructive since it is ultimately unsustainable and can lead to exhaustion and burnout.

It is a natural reflex for a leader to want his or her people to be pulling their weight and sharing the burdens of office. An interesting illustration from the pre-email era can be found in Robert Jackall's 1988 work *Moral Mazes: The World of Corporate Managers.* Jackall spent a considerable period with a large US conglomerate, which he referred to pseudonymously as Covenant Corporation:

'The story is told in Covenant Corporation about how the CEO was distressed, upon first taking power, to find no-one at work when he reached corporate headquarters at his accustomed hour of 6.30am. He remedied the loneliness of the situation by leaving notes on the desks of all his top executives saying, "Call me when you get in."'

The impact of this is entirely predictable – of course, the email has replaced the note on the desk. So sending a message out at 6.30am or on a weekend from your BlackBerry to all your direct reports is a sure-fire way of testing who is on top of their messages, who is on the case. Because email can multiply as it trickles down the organisation, the impact of this behaviour can be to generate no end of unproductive activity which achieves little more than an opportunity for people to signal their presence, whether real or virtual. This virtual presenteeism can become pervasive to such an extent that out-of-hours communication becomes normalised, something by no means limited to an organisation's leadership. This need to signal one's presence and to demonstrate that one is "on the case" leads to the habitual "firing from the hip" that often becomes established as part of an email culture. In this context, the act of replying – and being seen to reply – is more important than the content of the message. Inevitably, recipients of messages reply quickly without having read the message in full, leading to misunderstandings, further work and yet more emails.

Knowing what to cut out

Almost as important as knowing what to do as a manager and leader is knowing what not to do. Practically cutting out the 80 per cent of activity that will only yield 20 per cent of the impact makes sense but is tricky to do in practice. One of the poorer bosses I had was often too busy to see his own people, usually because he was afraid of confronting them over some issue he had failed to support them on. By door-stepping him at his office, I got a picture of some of the meetings he was attending. I found him giving a full hour to people *I* had declined to see. He was totally indiscriminate with his time, which had the knock-on impact of making him less available for his own people, something which was not altogether accidental.

Be ruthless with meetings

It is now common practice to look at mobiles and BlackBerrys covertly during meetings, something that most people would acknowledge as rude but which, nevertheless, has become broadly accepted as inevitable. In conferences and seminars, laptops are commonplace, ostensibly to make notes during the conference; however, it is now not unusual at large business conferences to see row upon row of delegates looking at their email as a speaker addresses the room. In September 2009, a picture of the Connecticut legislature in the United States showed politicians playing solitaire and looking at news sites on their laptops during a session.

We have seen that published research shows pretty authoritatively that attempting to do two things at once means that we are not only likely to do one or both things poorly, but that we invoke the brain's self-defence mechanisms which impose limits on its processing ability. This means that even those games of solitaire may not get played as effectively as possible if legislators are trying to keep one eye on the business of the assembly.

If one is reduced to looking at a mobile, PDA or laptop in a meeting, it suggests one of three things: there are urgent things to be attended to outside the meeting; your presence at the meeting is unnecessary and you should not be there; your presence at the meeting is necessary but the meeting is being chaired poorly and your attention is drifting. Whichever the scenario, the effective thing to do is to either change the course of the meeting so that your time is being used effectively or leave the meeting as courteously as possible. If there is a section of the agenda that is only pertinent to a sub-set of attendees, it is perfectly legitimate to request that this be handled at the end of the meeting when other attendees have been excused. Even if a meeting is under way, it is better to either leave or end the meeting early than stay for a full hour or longer if there is no intention to follow up. It is much better to be direct with people and state diplomatically that you feel you have contributed as much as you can and then leave.

With meetings, prevention is better than cure and it is

far better to avoid the meeting in the first place. Of every meeting to which you receive an invite or that your P.A. or secretary pencils into the diary, ask how it can contribute to the handful of key objectives that will contribute to your great year. Even if it is one of those meetings, always ask yourself if it is better handled by one of your direct reports (we will discuss the importance of delegation shortly).

In large organisations, senior managers are in demand at any number of recurring meetings, if only to reassure others in attendance. Rather than refuse to attend or simply not turn up, it is better to excuse yourself having fed back to the meeting why you do not think it is a good use of your time to attend.

As with company-wide "email free" days, some corporates have introduced "meeting free" days. A human resources director at a top British retailer recently told me that they had recently "banned" meetings on Fridays in order to help people become more productive, focus on output and even clear emails. Meeting rooms normally being used from dawn to dusk were now empty on Fridays and senior managers entered the spirit of the initiative by cheerfully interrupting meetings on Fridays and, if necessary, physically dragging participants out. Unfortunately, in the experience of the HR director in question, this happened to her during a particularly sensitive personal discussion with a distressed employee. So, as with blanket email rules, the flexibility needed by the individual employee needs to be considered.

CHAPTER EIGHT

Leadership

"The fish rots from the head" – ancient Chinese saying

An organisation takes its cue from the leadership. Good and bad practices become established as habitual and, to an extent, we become inured to them. If you are in a chief executive or managing director role, you have the opportunity – and indeed a responsibility - to set the tone for your entire organisation. Even if you lead only a small team, it is still possible to agree with the people that work for you that you will work in a certain way.

If you feel that your organisation is working at about the right level and is being highly effective, then there is no need for action. If, however, levels of stress are high, people feel overwhelmed by the levels of emails and you sense poor levels of effectiveness, then there is the opportunity to address things. We have looked already at how use of communications technology can be tackled and at the importance of focus; in both of these areas, organisations take their cue from the top. This chapter addresses some of the other dimensions of leadership.

Communicating as Leader: Vision, Purpose and Stability

Most corporates are well-equipped when it comes to the infrastructure for internal communication, with larger organisations dedicating people within the Human Resources Department full-time to the activity. Most chief executives pay considerable attention to the establishment and communication of corporate ideals, objectives and the strategic plan. It is also important for managers and leaders of divisions and teams to provide a similar framework within their own teams. If this is done properly, people will have clarity about the direction the business is going in and their own role in it.

One aspect of corporate life that appears to be done less well is the management of bad news. This may take the form of poor results, financial difficulties or reorganisation. My view is that it pays to be as honest and direct with people as possible, even where this is uncomfortable; if the situation can be controlled, then communicate what you are doing about it. If aspects are outside your control, then say so and explain why. I have been thanked by people working for me for doing so in difficult situations. In an environment where people feel uncertain or vulnerable, they will instinctively revert to the well-established ancestral impulse of gossip.

The role of leader is often a rhetorical one. A further reason for a leader to refrain from the practice of originating large volumes of emails is that frenetic behaviour communicates to the organisation a sense of the jitters rather than one of a firm hand on the tiller. There are some situations where a little distance is conducive to a sense of personal stability.

Organisational stability is important also. I have come across few things as enervating to a business as an internal re-organisation. The process of organisational change has been studied in depth by business psychologists. American Kurt Lewin writing in the 1940s observed that change comprised three stages: Freeze, change and unfreeze. I would argue that there is an additional lengthy stage preceding a reorganisation in which people are unprofitably preoccupied with what shape the changes will take. A further stage after the re-organisation – euphemistically called "bedding down" – involves individuals trying to make sense of how they are now meant to work with one another. If at all possible, large-scale re-organisations should be avoided.

Setting the right tone as leader

An organisation's leader has an enormous responsibility when it comes to the context within which his or her people work.

We have seen evidence that in a culture in which email and BlackBerry use is not controlled, it becomes accepted practice to use a BlackBerry when in meetings even though most people would agree that this lacks courtesy and can have negative consequences for other meeting attendees.

While nobody wishes to run an organisation populated by indolent, complacent people, it is more likely that in today's workplace people will be working excessive hours and allowing work to intrude into family time in a way that is actually counter-productive.

What is rarely appreciated is that people's behaviour changes according to context, something observed by Malcolm Gladwell in *The Tipping Point.*[xlii] Gladwell cites the experiment conducted by American psychologists John M. Darley and C. Daniel Batson in the 1970s. Darley and Batson took 67 students at Princeton Theological Seminary and gave them a psychometric questionnaire on the nature of their religious belief gauging, for example, the extent to which they viewed religion as an end in itself or a means to a greater good. They then asked some of them to prepare a brief career talk to a group of students in a nearby building and the remainder to prepare a talk on the parable of the Good Samaritan. You may remember the biblical parable in which Jesus explains how a man is robbed and left for dead on the way from Jerusalem to Jericho; a priest and a high-status Levite cross the road to avoid the victim while the lowly Samaritan stops to take care of him.

In the experiment, a staged "victim" placed himself in an alley on the way to the venue for the talk and the researchers measured the reaction of the students as they made their way over. The interesting dimension is that a subset of the students was abruptly told that they were running late and that they needed to hurry. The results are striking. Of those not urged to hurry, 63 per cent stopped to help the "victim" in some way; only ten per cent of those urged to hurry did so. Extraordinarily, the researchers found that "on several occasions, a seminary student going to give his talk on the parable of the Good Samaritan literally stepped over the victim as he hurried on his way!"[xliii] There was no significant difference in behaviour either as a function of subject matter of the talk or as a function of the nature of the subject's religious belief. As Gladwell concludes: "The only thing that really mattered was whether the student was in a rush."

So simply telling somebody to hurry can completely alter their propensity to act in a charitable or altruistic way, even when the parable of the Good Samaritan should be foremost in their minds. This is what Gladwell refers to as the "power of context" and is a reminder that we are not fixed in our personalities or our behaviours, but often subject to the forces at work in our environment.

We are psychologically "wired" to come to swift conclusions about people and situations. There appear to be good evolutionary reasons for this to do with survival and its dependence on drawing rapid conclusions as to whether someone or something is kin, friend or threat. This means that we are driven to make psychological short-cuts about people and situations, something psychologists refer to as heuristics. We tend to make swift conclusions about people and attribute their behaviour to a fixed personality; we will conversely underplay contextual factors which is why we find the results of the Good Samaritan experiment so striking. Again, psychologists have done a good deal of work on this over the last 30 years or so following the early research by Lee Ross in 1977 of the concept of Fundamental Attribution Error. In the world of business psychology, this has been used principally to address selection and assessment, something that has become big business for work psychologists. In the context of a job interview or an assessment centre, FAE needs to be understood alongside a range of other psychological processes that may cloud our judgement when recruiting or assessing an individual – a candidate may appear nervous in a job interview, but this does not necessarily reflect their performance once in a job.

If we accept that we are prone to underestimate the impact of environmental or contextual factors in an individual's behaviour, there is something of a vacuum in applying this to leadership. If, as is often the case, an organisation's leadership is doing the equivalent of telling people that they are running late, then this is going to have a negative impact on both the effectiveness of their work and the way in which they treat others around them. What the Good Samaritan experiment suggests is that our sense of human decency is not fixed but is very fragile, and can be swept away in certain environmental conditions even when the merits of helping out a stricken individual should be foremost in our mind.

So when I talk of setting the right tone, I am thinking not just of how a culture of measured, effective focus can deliver more than one of frenetic urgency in which everybody is spread too thinly. I am also thinking of the moral framework, a sense of decency and the establishment of traditional virtues in the way we work with one another.

Decency is not a word used with great frequency in the business world, but I believe that it is an important component in an organisation's climate and something that the leader has a responsibility to ensure exists. Without it, poor behaviour abounds with detrimental effects upon people's commitment to the organisation and their morale. We have already seen the extent to which it has become acceptable to look at a BlackBerry during a meeting with colleagues. I cited the research conducted by Glenn Wilson that showed 90 per cent of subjects believing that it was rude to check emails in meetings, but a third believing that it had become "acceptable and seen as a sign of diligence and efficiency". We have already covered the reasons why such behaviour may lead to reduced efficiency, but the consensus that "rude" behaviour has become acceptable is possibly more depressing still.

I see something of a backlash in evidence among some business people. Entrepreneur Luke Johnson wrote in *The Times* in June 2009:

"I was recently reprimanded for peeking at [my BlackBerry] during a board meeting – a gross form of hypocrisy on my part, because I once threatened to sling out of the window any PDA-type devices being used in meetings I chaired. I have now vowed to switch off both BlackBerry and mobile in all meetings – anything less is uncivil."[xliv]

I believe it to be telling that a high profile entrepreneur such as Johnson refers to a lack of civility. Civility is, after all, a near-forgotten Victorian virtue so why should the Chairman of a twenty-first century broadcaster feel the need to invoke it? I believe that this sense of decency in our behaviour to one another is about more than behaviour in meetings. I remember a Chief Executive in a large corporation for which I worked pulling together his 50 most senior managers and explaining that, following a recent visit to a provincial company site, he had received complaints about long-standing problems with the toilets on the premises; it seemed that nobody had been able or had had the will to navigate the bureaucracy sufficiently effectively to get them fixed. The CEO naturally got the issue fixed and received a number of letters of thanks from staff at the site. He then delivered a coruscating rebuke to his team of senior managers about the fact that junior staff had felt compelled to write to him to thank him for doing something so basic as getting the toilets fixed. He presented this as a symptom of a fundamental failure to look after our people.

Other dimensions of personal decency include the way we treat one another when we communicate whether electronically or in face-to-face meetings. I am thinking here not just of colleagues but also customer and suppliers. One of the side-effects of the burgeoning volume of emails experienced by so many in corporate life is that it has lowered the level of what has become acceptable in day-to-day contact with other people. Because volumes of emails are becoming unmanageable, it has become normal practice a) not to reply to incoming messages unless the recipient perceives it useful to do so, and b) to try and cope with some of the volume by managing emails during meetings.

In the excellent October 2009 post on boston.com titled "Timely Tips to Empty your In-box," the author Scott Kirsner interviews a number of CEOs to get their insights on staying on top of your in-box. Kirsner asks Gail Goodman, chief executive of email marketing firm Constant Contact, how she deals with the guilt of not replying to all her messages. She replies:

"I used to try to be polite to everybody but then I got over the need to respond to someone I've never heard of who is trying to sell me something."[xlv]

This is a small but powerful illustration of the findings of Batson's Good Samaritan experiment. Pressure of time and the sheer volume of emails is, according to Goodman's personal testimony, directly responsible for her sacrificing courtesy. The worry here is what else will she and her peer group ultimately also "get over" not doing – having meetings with direct reports? Reading bed-time stories to kids? It demonstrates the extent to which guilt is entirely relative and can be readily suppressed when we are under time pressure. Guilt, like embarrassment, is a sensation designed to prevent us from doing socially unacceptable things in our ancestral environment and thus becoming shunned and less likely to survive and reproduce. But in today's global digital community, we make the calculation – probably correctly – that, on balance, the volume of people available to us to meet and do business with is so large that we can drop social niceties with little consequence.

This behaviour with email and in meetings lacks courtesy and also alienates the person on the receiving end, particularly when they may have gone to some trouble to compose the message or preparing for a meeting in the first place. In both cases, this behaviour tends to take hold when the recipient of the message or the BlackBerry user is of higher status than the sender or the meeting attendee. This may be a function of the person's place in an organisation's hierarchy or it may be a customer–supplier relationship. I have been on both sides of the buyer–supplier relationship and it is very easy and quick to provide unsuccessful suppliers with a quick response. Treating people with courtesy in all circumstances needs no other justification other than the fact that it happens to be the right and proper way to behave. There is also the "karmic" justification that people will remember the manner of your contact with them and the relationship may be inverted in a future encounter.

The concept of "values" is commonplace in business life – they are rarely just "values" and are usually "core values", implying the existence of another set of values that are non-core. In *Built to Last*, Mike Porras and Jerry Collins attribute much of the success of the "visionary" companies to a coherent set of values[xlvi]. The existence of the values appears to be more important than their actual nature, which can straddle corporate mission and objectives. But if we understand values to mean the moral principles that determine the way a company conducts itself, then it is indeed a fundamental component of an organisation's fabric and something a leader needs to drive hard. We have already looked at the use of a published and universally understood code to establish the boundaries around email use; the same approach is required for a broader set of boundaries around the way in which people work together. In one company, these values were listed on a framed document which was placed in every meeting room in the company. The values themselves ("We respect one another") were platitudinous but well-intentioned enough. However, they were so poorly adhered to – not least by the organisation's leadership - that people tended to mutter them with heavy sarcasm under their breath when colleagues signally failed to observe them. It is one thing to publish a set of values – it is another altogether to enforce them, and this is a further dimension of the function of the leader that we shall come to.

A key component in achieving focus and working effectively is people – getting the best out of them and ensuring they too are not labouring under stressful, unfocused, hyperactive conditions. It is also crucial in establishing the tone and sense of decency that you, as leader, would like to see in place throughout the organisation. People management has become something of a lost art – in the next chapter we examine why it is important and how it can be done well.

CHAPTER NINE

People

"Your most precious possession is not your financial assets. Your most precious possession is the people you have working there, and what they carry around in their heads, and their ability to work together."
(attributed to Robert Reich)

I cannot be alone in groaning inwardly each time I hear a corporate person express the sentiment "People are our most important asset" or that their most important assets leave in the lift each evening. It is almost never true – either literally or figuratively. However, my view is that how people are managed, led and developed is the single most important factor in creating an effective organisation rather than a collection of hyperactive ineffective individuals.

If you were to look at the published accounts of any the leading companies in the FTSE 100, you would be unlikely to find anything in the balance sheet that places a value on people. Attempts have, however, been made to introduce the concept of Human Capital Accounting in much the same way as brands have been valued as intangible assets. However, these have generally become mired in the difficulties of achieving this objectively in a way that can be written into accounting standards. Scandinavia is something of an exception. For example, Skandia publishes an intellectual capital supplement to its annual report; this at least establishes the principle of attributing a value to a company's intellectual resources.

While there has been a degree of academic and accounting debate as to how human capital can be reported upon, the reason the concept has not taken off is that shareholders and the investor community do not take it seriously, perhaps an indication of the short-termism for which the City is notorious. Certainly, my own experience as chief executive of a public company was that in numerous meetings with professional investors I was never asked about the way the company's people were managed, retained or developed. I was, however asked about "headcount" with questions exclusively around cost and any projected increases.

Managing and leading people properly is one of the first casualties of an over-active, trigger-happy, technology-overload culture. It is also a major part of the solution in putting that culture right.

Of the leaders I have worked with, I have always fared best under those that seemed to be in control of their day-to-day lives and were not being thrown from pillar to post on a daily basis by the sheer demands of their job. Of all the various people that I have worked for, only two fall into this category. The two were not wholly alike but both possessed a rare combination of ambition and laziness; the result of this combination was an uncanny knack at getting the best of the people that worked for them.

One of them had engineered my succession of his role when he was promoted into an overseas position. The advice he gave me as I took over an organisation of around one hundred people was to remind me that if I were to double my work-rate, I would only be lifting that of my organisation by a half of one per cent. The important thing to do was to leverage my organisation. I still come across senior managers today who have not grasped this.

1. Hire Great People

Before getting on to exactly how to leverage an organisation, one fundamental aspect of that organisation that has to be examined is the quality of the people. This is particularly the case with your direct reports. These should be the best people you can possibly lay your hands on. Having talented, capable, team-oriented people in your top team can make your own job infinitely easier. Of course, to get the best out of such a team, they need to be managed, led and developed in the right way, which we shall come on to. The first thing to look for is capability and ambition. A successful leader needs someone that is ultimately capable of taking over from him or her. Succession is something we shall cover shortly.

The second quality I look for in a direct report – and one of equal importance to their capability – is their ability to play as part of a team. We will come to the reasons why I put such emphasis on this, but it makes an enormous difference to the individual's effectiveness as part of your management team. To screen out inappropriate people, ask a lot of questions at interview about what obstacles they overcame in delivering their achievements; examples of internal conflict that they have encountered and how they dealt with it; evidence that they can work successfully within a team. Negative indicators to look out for include posturing that they single-handedly saved the company or delivered a major initiative; another is negative comments about peers or team-mates.

2. Promote from within

"Promote from within" is a battle-cry that rings out from *Built to Last* by Jerry Porras and James Collins. The book examines eighteen "visionary" companies that have sustained high performance over several decades, and establishes what distinguishes them from a control group of 18 comparison companies that have performed less well. Many of the virtues covered in the book, such as having a core set of values and pursuing "big hairy audacious goals", are consistent with the set of strategies required to eliminate unprofitable activity. Nowhere is this more the case than in the context of promoting from within.

This is the one area where there is arguably the starkest divide between the visionary companies and the comparators, particularly where it examines the hiring of CEOs. It is also one of the most tangible recommendations and, in contrast to near-truisms such as "preserve the core", can be examined with real data. The book includes a table showing which companies put outsiders into the role of chief executive between 1806 and 1992. Strikingly, 13 of the 18 comparison companies had done so; this contrasts with only two for the visionary companies. To express the data in another way, the authors add:

"across *seventeen hundred years* of combined history in the visionary companies, we found only *four* individual cases of an outsider coming directly into the role of chief executive"(italics are the authors').

One of the two visionary companies to have hired an external CEO is, interestingly, Disney which recruited Michael Eisner as CEO and which went into rapid decline after the book's publication. We have referred already to Eisner's frenetic work schedule. After pulling off a small number of high-impact initiatives at Disney in the early years of his tenure, he went on to hire and then dramatically fall out with Jeffrey Katzenberg and Michael Ovitz; the former left to co-found Dreamworks, which has become a formidable competitor to Disney. Eisner left the company by agreement in 2005 following interventions by Walt Disney's nephew Roy, who accused him of micromanagement, a style that is consistent with Eisner's hyperactivity.

The mantra of "promote from within" is rarely heard even 15 years after the publication of *Built to Last*. Now, we are more likely to read about the "War for Talent" following the 1998 McKinsey Quarterly article of that name. Interestingly, the article itself is mostly about *retention* of talent but the phrase has, in the language of business psychologists, entered the discourse and, as a consequence, business are performing discursively and hiring like mad. "The Secrets of CEOs", co-authored by the managing partner of a leading headhunter, has no coverage of talent management and talks dramatically of the "World War for Talent" in an interpretation of the phrase that is exclusively focused on recruitment.

Other positive examples from *Built to Last* include Procter & Gamble which, Dun's Review once commented, had "talent stacked like cordwood". Porras and Collins attribute the benefits of hiring leaders from within to the continuity of the company's core ideology. While this is undoubtedly the case, the practice also helps avoid much of the disruption caused by hiring outsiders. While I am not suggesting that CEOs recruited from outside will inevitably be hyperactive or micromanaging failures, the data suggests that they are at the very least likely to be divisive. Externally hired CEOs will initially feel alienated by the culture of the organisation they join and will miss the trusted lieutenants that were a part of their prior success. One of their first acts in a new role is often hiring of these lieutenants. They in turn will want to make an impact and hire people of their own. All this risks displacing and demotivating capable and long-serving people within the company.

3. Have a Succession Plan for Everybody

To execute the "promote from within" principle, you need to plan succession. It's important to do this not just for CEOs but for all levels, since internal promotion tends to leave a gap. Whenever I was involved in a discussion over whom should be promoted into a vacant position, one of the first questions that would be asked would be, "Is there an obvious successor to replace him/her?" While an insecure manager might feel threatened by a direct report that is capable of succeeding him, the smart boss knows that this actually makes him easier to promote. It is also good practice as managers occasionally fall ill or even die suddenly.

Done properly, succession is planned into an organisation. It does not necessarily have to revolve around one individual. In fact, this can backfire, creating a sense of entitlement in the individual in question and signalling to his or her peers that they may be best advised looking for another job.

4. Make Your People Work as a Team
(Why being likened to ferrets in a sack is a bad thing)

My experience is that *nothing* holds an organisation back and soaks up energy more than in-fighting. It does not need to be a large organisation for it to take root as even a small team can be disrupted by dysfunctional behaviour. For a leader, this can be doubly draining on time and energy as a) the effectiveness of your organisation is reduced, and b) you will be drawn directly into mediating between rival factions, usually in the form of your direct reports. I never cease to be amazed at the extent to which in-fighting and internal politics, like a surplus of emails, are widely accepted as an inevitable part of day-to-day working life. At one extreme, this became externally exposed to such an extent in one company that I worked for that one business journalist likened its senior management behaviour to that of "ferrets in a sack". If, as was the case here, direct reports of the group chief executive were briefing against one another in the press, then something is seriously wrong.

I would argue that endemic in-fighting is a more serious issue than overall staff performance, since even capable people will have their efforts diverted if their boss is part of a wider political struggle. If capable people are unable to deliver because another part of the company is deliberately withholding cooperation, then it can be sufficiently demotivating for them to consider leaving. An extreme example in my experience was being tasked with setting up a division to sell a new product and pre-selling it to a large corporate only to find that they had already been contacted by another part of my company which had set up a rival product. This was done with the sponsorship of a senior manager in another division who regarded the initiative as incursion into his divisional territory and disliked me personally from his time as my line manager. While everybody agreed that this was absurd behaviour, nobody was fired or reprimanded – the issue was simply ducked at a series of non-confrontational meetings.

Tribalism is a natural human impulse that evolutionary psychology can throw some light on. The impulse is clear to modern observers of hunter-gather societies. In *The Descent of Man* Darwin wrote: "The tribes inhabiting adjacent districts are almost always at war with each other.." and yet "a savage will risk his own life to save that of a member of the same community." Jared Diamond, in *The Third Chimpanzee* describes his discipline of asking for permission to enter tribal territories when bird-watching in New Guineas; on the occasions that he has not done so or asked permission at the wrong village, he has been confronted by "canoes of stone-throwing villagers, furious that I had violated their territory." When living with the Elopi tribe in West New Guinea, Diamond expressed a wish to cross into the territory of the neighbouring Fayu tribe – he was told in a matter-of-fact way that the Fayus would kill him if he tried.[xlvii]

The impulse to remain steadfastly loyal to our kin or our immediate social group – and at the same time hostile to others – has stayed with us into the twenty-first century. It is obviously present among sports fans, nationalists, political activists and religious factions all over the world. What typifies followers in these contexts is often the vehemence with which they oppose those from the other factions with the greatest vehemence of all reserved for anybody who crosses from one to another. In the heat of this opposition, depth of feeling is usually such that both sides sincerely regard the other as being genuinely wrong in some way and pursue their opposition with self-righteous vigour.

However, psychology can also throw light on this sort of bias. In her book *The Nurture Assumption*[xlviii], Judith Rich Harris draws on research into the arbitrariness of tribal rivalry among children conducted by Henri Tajfel in Bristol in the 1970s. Tajfel took two groups of 14- and 15-year-old schoolboys and individually asked them to guess the number of dots in visual clusters flashed before them. This was a mock "visual judgement" exercise in which the guessing was of no consequence. Tajfel then randomly allocated each boy to one of two groups – underestimators and overestimators. Each boy was told which group he belonged to and was then asked to complete a reward sheet suggesting how much money should go to each boy; identities were hidden but it was clear which of the two groups the boys belonged to. The result was that the boys gave more money to their own group and less to the other in spite of the arbitrariness of the grouping. As Tajfel concluded: "Apparently, the mere fact of division into groups is enough to trigger discriminatory behaviour."[xlix]

The truth is that in any given tribal situation, we will always believe ourselves to be slighted in some way, and we will always believe that those in the rival faction have been guilty of some form of underhand or immoral behaviour. While this may often be with justification, the truth is often more neutral since we are psychologically conditioned to think the worse of those outside our own faction. In our ancestral environment, a strong sense of kinship and the resulting willingness to fight for one another, was clearly central to our survival.

As humans, we have an extraordinary capacity for selectiveness in judging our own actions and those of others. It is therefore entirely natural and consistent with our psychological make-up to fall into some sort of tribalism in our work lives. It is important to negate the effects of this in your organisations.

I have seen a number of ineffectual attempts to tackle this issue:

• publishing a set of "values", the first of which is "we are one company". This is muttered with increasing cynicism as the spirit is contravened with impunity.

- Stickers with "One (insert company name)" plastered on the walls of the building, including toilet cubicles.
- A senior management internal conference where an internal manager notorious for Machiavellian in-fighting repents in a *mea culpa* staged interview.

All such initiatives are doomed to fail in an environment where in-fighting continues to be tolerated. It starts with the leadership of an organisation, and zero-tolerance is the only answer.

4.1 Structure the organisation for optimal unity: The Rule of 150
Size matters. In *The Tipping Point*, Malcolm Gladwell examined the psychological properties of groups of certain sizes and how they could accelerate a newly published book towards the best-seller lists in the right circumstances. He examined the corporate experience of Gore Associates – the company behind Gore-Tex – in the context of organisational size. He quotes Wilbert "Bill" Gore, the founder of the company as saying in an interview some years previously: "We found again and again that things get clumsy at a hundred and fifty." Gore then pursued a strategy of having a maximum of 150 employees per plant. Gladwell quotes a current associate of the company as follows:

"People used to ask me, how do you do your long-term planning. And I'd say, that's easy, we put a hundred and fifty parking spaces in the lot, and when people start parking on the grass, we know it's time to build a new plant."

Gladwell suggests that the resulting cohesion and unity of each plant is a major contributor to Gore's sustained commercial success and its reputation as a desirable company to work for. He then examines the psychological drivers behind this phenomenon and, once again, there are clues in our ancestral environment. Anthropologist Robin Dunbar established the relationship among primates and humans between brain size – specifically that of the neocortex which is far larger than that of other mammals – and the average size of groups they live with. The size of the neocortex determines how many people an individual can remember and therefore sustain personal relationships with. Dunbar developed an equation for the correlation between the size of brain and social group and concluded that 150 was around the maximum size for humans. Dunbar himself observed that this was already evident in military structures because in a group of 150 or less, "orders can be implemented and unruly behaviour controlled on the basis of personal loyalties and direct man-to-man contacts." The fact that members of a group all know one another means that there is a disincentive to alienate others and social norms become easily enforced. As we saw earlier, our capacity for language – and hence gossip – distinguishes us from other primates not least by enabling us to thrive in a social group that is greater than 50. However, what Dunbar has established is that there is an upper limit in our ability to accommodate recognition of people, and this appears to be set at around 150.

Dunbar went on to establish, through an examination of a number of hunter-gather societies, that tribal groups tend to be an aggregation of a number of 150-member clans. This fundamental aspect of human mental capacity has important consequences for organisational structure. For teams or divisions that swell beyond 150 – be it in a corporate or social context – there appears to be an inevitable process of fragmentation with sub-groups or cliques appearing. So, as far as possible, organisational unity is best preserved *within* a given team by maintaining an upper limit of 150.

However, creating a tribal unity within one unit can have negative consequences if good relationships are required across "tribes". Gladwell reports the findings of another Gore associate that visits Lucent to find coherent groupings around vertical functions such as manufacturing or sales between which existed a paucity of personal relationships. He contrasted this with the plant structure of Gore where the sales and manufacturing staff were within the same group of 150.

There is clearly a dilemma for large organisations between deriving scale from large vertical functions and organisational coherence around individual business groups.

It is, of course, possible to establish "virtual teams" across organisational boundaries with good personal relationships. My experience, though, of large organisations is that functional divisions become divisive – people operate in silos and adversarial relationships develop where mutual support is required for the business to operate successfully. The organisation will invest enormous amounts of time and energy in efforts to improve customer experiences when confronted with cases of customers "falling between gaps" or becoming shunted between different parts of the organisation. The temptation is to externalise the issue and tinker with the "system". However, the fact is – and it remains under-appreciated – that most organisations are structured in a way that runs directly against the way in which the human brain is hardwired for optimal social performance.

4.2 Keep the emphasis on your external competitors

Nothing unites an organisation more than a threat from outside. One way to dilute internal tribalism is to emphasise the threat from external competition. This can take the form of communicating the activities of competitors such as new product launches and marketing campaigns. Team members should take an active role in understanding the threat from competition without being demoralised by it. Where appropriate, make it a requirement of all team members to acquire relevant competitive intelligence, for example publicly available pricing information or marketing material. Large organisations in particular can easily become inwardly-focused and complacent about external competition. Everybody in the company needs to be galvanised against the competition; where possible, team communication needs to include updates on market share and advances against others in the market. Team members need to understand the strengths and weaknesses of competitor products and the ways to sell their own company's products against them. It is worth establishing a small team of competitive intelligence analysts who are able to distribute information to the company.

If this is the context against which people work on a daily basis, it becomes harder for people to disrupt activity that will thwart the competition.

4.3 Be ruthless when it comes to in-fighting within your own team
When you hire people, particularly your top reports, get evidence of their credentials as a team player through rigorous interviews, references and possibly psychological profiling. If you do not entirely trust an interviewee's capacity for collegiate behaviour, do not offer them a job under any circumstances.

Where you have inherited direct reports, make it clear at the very outset that one of the values that you put most emphasis on in your people is their capacity to play as part of a team. It is also important to state as soon as possible that you observe a zero tolerance approach to in-fighting. Most people will respond to this once it is made clear. Unfortunately, for some it will prove impossible to change old habits.

For die-hard political operators, office life is a zero-sum game. If one of their peers succeeds, they feel that they will inevitably lose out. Try as you might to persuade them that a rising tide lifts all boats, they will find any number of ways in which to undermine their peers. One of these ways will inevitably become apparent in one-to-one conversations with you when they will take the opportunity to denigrate whichever peer or peers most threaten them. This may be presented as an issue which is preventing them from succeeding; alternatively, it may be presented simply as helpful information. In my experience, these outbursts are silenced pretty rapidly if you ask the question what the accused party made of this feedback when they received it. We shall come to the role of feedback, but it needs to be made very clear to your people that you will not tolerate negative briefing about colleagues. To me, this issue is of such importance that if someone cannot desist from this bad behaviour, then they need to find work elsewhere.

4.4 Make feedback a habit for everybody

Feedback is a fundamental tool for reducing in-fighting, but it is easier to talk about than do in practice. People naturally find it difficult to confront colleagues directly and pass on negative feedback. This is one area where I feel established tools readily made available by most Human Resources departments are highly effective and just need to be implemented effectively by managers. Some take the form of "360 Degree Feedback", anonymous electronic surveys. These can bring out some useful information, but if people fear that they cannot bring issues out directly, then the team has problems that no number of anonymous surveys can fix.

I have a strong preference for face-to-face feedback in all directions. This can be uncomfortable at first, particularly for an insecure leader with talented direct reports, but once established as a habit it will make an enormous contribution to the smooth running of the team. To kick-start this, it often helps to have an off-site meeting and make the feedback part of a broader team-building process. These "bonding" sessions are much pilloried but, if well-run, can be a valuable investment in your team's coherence. Taking a team out of the office and placing everyone in a different context allows everyone an insight into the broader aspects of colleagues' personalities and backgrounds. If the team combines to complete challenging physical tasks, whether it is raft-building or abseiling, trust between them will increase and they will find engaging aspects of one another's personalities. Personal histories, anecdotes and sporting affiliations all tend to emerge and help transform all team members into three-dimensional human beings.

On their own, these team-building exercises are not enough as they are outside the context of the office. Once the team returns to the office, the context is changed and the camaraderie can quickly evaporate. The most effective team trips that I have been part of have included a large component of team-working in an office context.

One of the most valuable elements of this is a feedback exercise which, in ideal circumstances, is handled by an experienced facilitator and conducted off-site. The best exercise that I have been exposed to is very simple but highly effective. Every member of the team is given a stack of small cards; they are asked to complete a card for each member of the team with five points each under two headings:

1) Five things I really appreciate about you.
2) Five things I would like you to do differently.

Then each team member reads these out to the person concerned in front of the whole group. It is important that this process includes the team leader and it is also important that the process is sensitively facilitated, preferably by somebody outside the team.

People will find this difficult at first but it becomes easier. The exercise should not become shrouded in negativity as even people that have been at one another's throats find they can usually dig up something positive to say, even if it is slightly double-edged such as "I appreciate your passionate approach to your work," or "I admire your tenacity in getting things done." Often, the mere exercise of writing these points down causes people to see their colleagues in a completely different light. When coupled with a richer sense of them as individuals resulting from the trip itself, the feedback exercise should become constructive and collaborative.

Importantly, people will be told things about themselves and their impact on colleagues that will come as something of a surprise. I vividly remember the feedback I received from our Human Resources manager which, delivered in a very measured way, made me realise that I had been unnecessarily hard on her when the policies she had to implement made little sense for my organisation. This made me think very hard about how I was treating individuals when frustrated by internal bureaucracy.

Once people have been eased into the environment of directly feeding back to one another, it is relatively simple to maintain it in an office environment. Once people have been open with another in a team context, it can become surprisingly habit-forming as long as the trust is maintained. Even when there is strong disagreement between members of the team, these can be discussed openly and collaboratively.

When giving feedback, it is important to restrict it to "clean" as distinct from "dirty" feedback in the parlance of organisational development professionals. Clean feedback is specific (i.e. relates to something tangible for which examples can be given) and actionable. Dirty feedback comprises negative sentiments that the recipient cannot easily address specifically, such as "You are not popular in the office," or "your work is often poor."

4.5 Handle conflict positively

An ideal team will have a mixture not just of functional skills (financial, technical, marketing) but also personalities, styles and outlooks. If everybody is irrepressibly optimistic all the time then there is the risk that a problem will go unnoticed; this is where it is helpful to have a balancing pessimist who has a "glass half-empty" view of life and will be more ready to play "devil's advocate" and voice concerns. This can be helpful in balancing the rest of the team.

If your direct reports have differing opinions about a significant business issue, their instinct will be to lobby you directly. As well as time-consuming, this can rapidly sour relations between peers who will wonder what exactly has been said behind closed doors to undermine their position. It very quickly becomes exposed to the rest of the organisation. I vividly remember a presentation from one of my team members to an approvals committee in a large company receiving an unexpectedly hostile reception from my boss at the time who chaired the committee. He asked some very negative questions of the presenter, which prompted another of my direct reports to lean across and whisper to me – rightly as it turned out – that one of my peers had "got to him first", i.e. lobbied our boss before the meeting.

This behaviour is destructive in a number of ways. It undermines the position of the manager who has not been lobbying his boss and exposes this fact to that manager's people. They in turn become distracted from their job and lose confidence in their boss's ability to manage the politics of the issue. Peers lose trust in one another and fail to cooperate on other objectives. Worst of all, they will get sucked up into a briefing arms-race in which everyone feels they need to get their boss on-side; relationships between team-mates become adversarial and they become motivated to sabotage one another's initiatives. The impact on the boss is enormous since not only will objectives start to be missed, but he will find himself besieged by his direct reports lobbying on a one-to-one basis.

To avoid this, bosses need to impose the discipline of forcing such issues into the open to be discussed as a team.

You will know when your direct reports are working effectively as a team. I knew I had got something right when I saw my Finance and Technical directors sit down together in a meeting room and work on something for a good hour and a half. When they emerged, I asked if everything was alright. "We had a bit of a problem," one of them said. "But we've figured out how to fix it." As chief executive, I was blissfully unaware of the problem until it had been fixed. Since the finance function of an organisation can often end up – often out of necessity – working in an adversarial way with other parts, this could have easily become a source of conflict. These become doubly hard work for the chief executive to resolve as he has to understand the business issues as well as navigate the personal and political dimensions to the resulting conflict.

5. Revive the Lost Art of Delegation

Delegation is a capability gap for many senior managers; this has been caused by a number of factors but I see largely as a collision of the fashion for flattened hierarchies and the growth of communications technology.

The stuffy, hierarchical offices of the past were undoubtedly a bad thing: executives tucked away in closed offices were inevitably out of touch with the "coal-face" and it became very difficult for individuals to challenge the received wisdom. The fashion for flattened hierarchies has yielded some excellent changes, such as the move away from offices towards open plan work areas which, done well, improve communication and can help with team-working. It is also increasingly the trend for senior managers to do away with the need for a dedicated personal secretary and share that person more widely with the team. Allan Leighton, Chairman of the Royal Mail, is an example of someone who projects this attitude in a very winning way in media interviews – where there has been a controversy concerning an individual postman, he has accompanied that person on their round.

While a manager of the 1960s Post Office would have shuddered at the idea of accompanying a postman on their round, it is possible that modern managers have taken the lack of hierarchy too far the other way and lost many of the benefits.

Having a personal secretary – even if this person is not dedicated to you – has a massive impact on effectiveness. This is particularly the case with diary management and fielding messages to other team members when you are out of the office.

Having a physical office should not be something to be embarrassed about even though there is a vague egalitarian trend that suggests it is bad practice. Where I have seen personal offices eradicated to very senior levels, the effectiveness of top managers is reduced as they find themselves scrabbling around for a quiet corner of the canteen in which to conduct a confidential meeting. When they inevitably get their secretaries to block book public meeting rooms for them, it causes more bad feeling than their prior possession of a private office. Offices are a good thing – they should also be made available to others when the main occupant is out.

The trend towards flattening of hierarchies has been

accelerated by the technology revolution; leaders can now see and manage their own diaries, respond directly to emails and return messages. This has caused the art of delegation to have been lost to many. In the high-octane world of instant e-mail, leaders become drawn into activity themselves where in a gentler age, they would have passed communications on to their key people to act upon. By not delegating in a measured and considered way, leaders commonly cut across their people or fail to direct them properly, frequently firing from the hip in an ineffective frenzy.

We have also lost the "chain of command", an expression rarely heard outside US police dramas such as *The Wire*. Even here, the context is usually around an officer bypassing an immediate superior and lobbying a senior. The chain of command, observed well, is a tool of effective management; if every small detail involves a chief executive who is copied on and replies to each email, the result may be a bad decision, but the practice also generates a lot of ineffective activity. The likelihood is that junior employees have a far deeper understanding of the issues and, if trusted and empowered, can make the right decision in any given situation. If emails are flying around from the chief executive involving each intermediate person in the hierarchy, each person in the chain feels obliged to contribute as part of the culture of conspicuous hyperactivity. The junior manager then becomes drawn into briefing upwards often through a poor medium, email. If the junior manager were trusted to make the decision correctly in the first place, the amount of time and energy saved for all involved is considerable. The trend towards hyperactive micromanagement erodes the investment of trust in our employees.

My personal epiphany about the power of delegation came when my first wife abruptly left me and our pre-school child. This turned out to be a hugely positive event for me personally as I soon met someone who became my second wife, and I was ultimately much happier. Professionally, I feared disaster initially as I had hitherto worked at least a 50-hour week and had always been at my desk by 7.45am, rarely leaving before 6pm in the evening. Now I was having to drop my chid off at nursery for 8am and pick him up by 6pm; so I was having to limit myself to a "nine-to-five" day.

I was fortunate in having a supportive boss who advised me to delegate heavily. I pulled my direct reports into my office and was candid with them. They too were supportive and so, out of necessity, I began to follow my boss's advice and put as much as possible on the shoulders of my direct reports. At that first meeting, I stated earnestly that I would be online from home in the evenings and able to continue work. In practice, once I had successfully acquired the delegation habit, I almost never switched my computer on in the evening. My direct reports took care of everything, leaving me to focus on the big issues and on coaching them. It struck me as a huge irony at the time that something that should have been a domestic disaster turned out to be an epiphany in effective leadership, one from which I have never looked back.

The best bosses I have worked for not only picked their key people carefully but also delegated heavily. In some instances, this was genuinely a function of their laziness as they wanted to do as little work themselves as possible. Cynical as this may sound, it made them better people to work for as they were clear-headed and were highly effective at upward management. By trusting their direct reports to get on with their jobs, they freed them up to be creative; because they were not immersed in detail, they were clear-headed enough to offer fresh insights when help was actually needed. Clear-headedness and perspective are among the first casualties of hyperactivity in senior managers.

The mantra of weary corporate men is that "shit runs downhill" – the flipside of delegation is protecting your direct reports from activity that prevents them from doing their jobs properly. A truly effective leader conserves their energies for managing the demands of their own boss. The worst boss I have ever worked for was frenetic, insecure and desperate to appear in a good light with his own boss. This led to a massive amount of work that had no impact on the company as it was geared towards either reducing his anxiety or ensuring that he would have a ready answer to absolutely anything he might be asked. If anything urgent or negative cascaded down to him, it would lead to a frenzy of activity. Someone once said to me, "shit runs downhill in his organisation," – the first time I had come across this charming phrase.

There are some bosses with whom it is simply impossible to build a good working relationship. Where someone is consistently overactive and inefficient in the way in which they cascade work, it suggests an inability to delegate and a possible lack of trust. Ironically, one of the possible ways to remedy this is to try to take as much work as possible away from the boss. He should, after all, regard it as a success if good people lower down his organisation can run with pieces of work and deal with them successfully.

It is also important to protect your own team of direct reports from the vagaries of a poor boss. Because of the boss's heightened status, your reports will be anxious to please him or her and so inbound requests will raise anxiety, generate frenetic activity and, in all likelihood, distract them from something more important. Again, wresting as much work from your boss as possible will help with this. Occasionally, it will be necessary to "fall on a grenade" and take the impact of something dramatic without distracting your team.

In terms of structure, having the right number of direct reports is also important. Everyone naturally wants to report to the boss, but there is an upper limit to the number of people that can be managed effectively in a leadership team. My preferred upper limit is six.

6. Make "Fluffy HR Stuff" Your Priority

Starting out as a chief executive of a joint venture, one of the first things I did was sit down my operations director for what my previous employer had called a "one-to-one". I explained that this was a monthly meeting at which we would, in addition to discussing objectives, discuss non-operational issues such as personal development and feedback. "Oh, right," she said, having admitted that she'd never had this sort of meeting before. "All the fluffy HR stuff."

As I got to know her previous manager better, it became less of a surprise that this was new to her. But in an environment where activity is directly correlated with status, managers commonly do not make time for sitting down with their direct reports either as individuals or teams. In the midst of a testosterone-fuelled frenzy, one-to-ones, appraisals and team meetings are regarded – even by female managers – as a rather effeminate extension of the Human Resources administrative function. And yet, this is one area where making an effort and being proactive makes your team run more effectively and ultimately save you from unproductive activity.

6.1 Have regular one-to-ones

One-to-one briefings should be a diarised monthly meeting which should include a review of objectives, personal development, feedback and any other issues on the mind of either participant.

If the discipline of focus outlined in Chapter Four is applied to your direct reports as effectively as you apply it to yourself, then your direct report will only be expending effort on a small number of big things. If those things are genuinely big, the chances are that you will be up to date with their progress to some extent. So the one-to-one meeting should include some coaching around the achievement of those objectives.

If things are going well, however, you should be able to spend the lion's share of the meeting on non-operational issues. This should include feedback in both directions, something that is easier if you have already conducted a kick-off feedback exercise as outlined in Chapter Nine. If you have established a good rapport and level of trust with your direct report, you should be able to give honest and direct feedback without them reacting negatively or becoming defensive.

There will inevitably be an area in which your direct report's performance could be better. The one-to-one is an opportunity to provide some coaching. It may take the form of feedback around an important presentation or meeting that you both attended. If you also seek feedback from your own peers as to how they regard your direct reports, you will be able to pass that on to them in these meetings.

I have known these meetings to be managed formally with agendas and notes. My preference is for informal meetings without notes. If the level of trust is where it needs to be for these meetings to be genuinely effective, then my belief is that there is no need for notes which simply add to the administrative burden and inhibit the openness of the discussion.

6.2 Take appraisals seriously

Appraisals are enormously important events for your people and among the first things to be delayed, compromised or forgotten altogether when managers are too "busy". Given their importance to your people, these need to be important to you if you are to get the best out of your team. In a corporate environment, you should never be too busy for appraisals.

These are an opportunity to give formal and explicit feedback on performance. An indication of the failure on the part of the appraising manager is if the outcome is a surprise to the person on the receiving end. This suggests that feedback has not been in place. If performance issues have made themselves apparent, then these should have been addressed over the course of monthly one-to-one meetings.

There are widely varying views as to what form the

appraisal should take. I believe that the most important aspect is that it happens at all. I think it is legitimate to ask employees to draft a review of themselves ahead of the meeting. This means that the session itself is a discussion of the review and an agreed position at the end which will be written up by the reviewing manager.

6.3 Put Personal Development Plans in place

Taking an active interest in your people's personal development is good practice and, if it improves their performance in their current role, will pay for itself several times over.

One can take the view that losing good people is to be avoided at all costs and that you should cling to them as tenaciously as possible. My personal view is that if you pursue what is right for the individual, then it will come good for you and your team. There is little point in having someone work for you if their aspirations are not being fulfilled and they are not happy on a day-to-day basis. If they have a career plan which involves them moving to another part of the company or outside altogether, then your help with that plan will, if anything, enhance their loyalty and performance for the remainder of their time with you. From a self-interest perspective, having a friendly former employee in the right place internally or externally can be very helpful in all sorts of circumstances.

Once you get a reputation for helping your direct

reports progress in their careers, you will be regarded as a good person to work for. This will in turn cause you to attract the best people.

If you have a training budget, use it. Even large corporates provide little formal training in basic management. Some high-quality coaching can improve an individual's level of confidence and performance. Many young managers feel ill-at-ease making formal presentations to large or senior audiences. This is a useful application of training budget and can be performed as a team exercise with feedback and mutual support.

Some human resources departments introduce mentoring programmes, something I counsel against. Mentoring is, in essence, a natural process in which young high-potential individuals and older, senior managers are drawn to one another – the former gets sponsorship and the benefit of experience; the latter gets the satisfaction of helping someone and a possible future ally. The attachment – sometimes unconsciously – of a young promising protégé to an experienced sympathetic mentor is a *symptom* of high performance behaviour. However, it is sometimes treated as causal with the contrived pairing off of individuals. When this happens, what results is rarely mentoring and is closer to coaching or counselling. This rarely works and can sometimes backfire if arranged "mentorships" cross gender or ethnic boundaries, as shown in the research paper "Dysfunctional Mentoring Relationships and Outcomes" published by psychologist Terri Scandura in the *Journal of Management*[1].

6.4 Have regular team meetings

A sign of the frenetic but ineffectual leader is their level of commitment to team meetings. I have seen senior directors in corporates arrange full team meetings, make an opening speech and then leave for the rest of the day. This sends a terrible message to team members: that the leader has more important things to do than spend the day with the team.

It is immeasurably important to spend time with your team and communicate with them openly. This includes your top level of direct reports and your team as a whole. Monthly team meetings with your management team are an opportunity for your community of direct reports to discuss issues as a team. This offers a good opportunity for you as a leader to measure how effectively they are working together as a team. A worrying sign is one of your direct reports approaching you before a meeting in order to influence the outcome. This is one of the negative behaviours that needs to be stopped with a zero tolerance approach. One of the ways that this sort of in-fighting can be resisted is to ensure that regular team meetings are happening and that they are effective. If something is agreed or decided at a meeting, it should be adhered to and respected by everybody.

Pulling together the whole organisation, as far as is

practically possible, is also important for communicating the key aspects of what you are trying to achieve as a team. It is an opportunity to articulate your values, vision and key objectives. It allows a wider group of people working for you to meet you first hand and hear directly from you what is important. It is also an opportunity to reward people for outstanding achievements.

6.5 Ensure clarity of roles and objectives
Care needs to be taken that team members not only have clarity in their objectives but also that there is no ambiguity in the relationship between their job and that of others. This can become fraught in large organisations where divisions can set up functions that rival existing ones in other divisions. I have known two senior managers with near-identical job titles go through internal meetings with each other in order to agree where one job began and the other ended. This is demoralising as well as hugely inefficient. It is ultimately for an organisation's leadership to establish a zero tolerance policy towards internal rivalry but every manager and leader needs to ensure that role ambiguity is eliminated as far as possible from their organisation.

Likewise, clarity of objectives is important for a number of reasons. Firstly, it is a means of enforcing focus so that an individual does not spread themselves too thin with several pages of complex but low-impact objectives, as I was tempted to do. Secondly, clarity of objectives is important in motivating the individual if this is clearly tied to incentives such as a bonus.

6.6 Enforce the fluffy HR stuff throughout your organisation
It is one thing to establish the discipline of good people management practice for your direct reports. It is equally important to enforce this throughout the community of people that work for you. You will inevitably have direct reports that are capable and bright but who may be poor people managers. They may have been promoted rapidly and often above older colleagues who have worked longer in their given areas. It is not uncommon for these managers to lack confidence in dealing with their people, and this is an important area of activity for you as a leader to engage with them.

There are a number of ways in which you can help ensure that your direct reports are performing optimally as managers and leaders. We have mentioned the provision of good quality external coaching where this is needed. It is also important to provide direct coaching as a manager. One important function is to attend the team meetings of your direct reports. This is something that I see happening very rarely but is good practice. It gives you an opportunity to see how your direct report is performing as a leader and how they interrelate with their own direct reports. It also gives you an opportunity to hear directly from people lower down the organisation and for them to hear from you.

An organisation that does not succumb to frenetic use of communications technology, does not have a meretricious long-hours culture and genuinely empowers people through delegation can be a great place to work, and can liberate the leader to achieve greater things not just at work but also in his or her personal life.

CHAPTER TEN

Freedom From Hyperactivity: The Virtuous Circle

"When a man is wrapped up in himself,
he makes a pretty small package" – John Ruskin

Once an organisation has an effective code in place for managing communications technology and once a leader has implemented high performance people-management practices throughout the hierarchy, the vicious cycle of hyperactivity, micromanagement and long hours will be put into reverse. Instead, the leader can focus on important issues, delegate effectively and get the best out of the organisation through investing time and energy in people.

Focusing on a small number of important things and getting the best out of your people can become habits. Once habituated to these practices, you will find a surprising amount of time freed up. If you are currently in the throes of coping with several hundred emails a day, this may seem like a distant dream, but there should come a point when you will wonder exactly how you will fill your day.

Do Lunch

I am a great believer in having lunch and lament the Anglo-Saxon habit of eating a sandwich at the desk while one hand taps away at the keyboard. It is a poor way to eat and while it probably does not cause lasting physiological harm, it can't be great for the digestion. Also, it is more or less impossible to enjoy food in this way. Lunch should be a pleasure, even if it is only a modest meal. Anecdotally, colleagues of mine that have worked in France, where mealtimes are generally treated with some reverence, tell me that it is unheard of for people to eat at their desks. At lunchtime, all staff regardless of seniority, sit together and eat either a packed lunch or a cooked meal. I have worked at some companies where the chief executive has made a habit of eating lunch in the staff canteen. This is an effective way of getting feedback from rank-and-file employees, and they in turn are impressed by the approachability of their boss.

Lunch is also an opportunity to build relationships whether with internal colleagues, customers or suppliers. The aphorism that "people do business" risks being forgotten – just as we naturally side with people with whom we have formed some form of tribal association, we will inevitably go out of our way to help someone with whom we have established a good personal relationship. In terms of evolutionary psychology, this has been described by Nigel Nicholson as "as kin", i.e. a surrogate for kinship. This used to be the way that business was done – it is now becoming scarcer due to the way in which time has become constrained by both the volume of work and the stigma attached to taking time out for a meal during the working day. My observation in recent years is that a lunch meeting, to the extent that it happens at all, will often get rescheduled or cancelled. When it does happen, one or both participants will interrupt the meal to make or receive mobile phone calls or deal with emails on their BlackBerrys.

It is something of a sad sign of the times that one even has to suggest this as a business practice as it was not long ago that business was done very much in this way; it is arguable that 20 years ago, good personal relationships were often so well-established that, on occasion, they clouded sound commercial judgement. But for key suppliers or major customers, the establishing of a personal relationship with a decision-making individual through which shared interests can be identified can make an enormous difference at difficult points in the future when some sort of service blip has occurred or a competitor attempts to wrest business away. Sales people are traditionally very good at this sort of activity, but they never perform better than when chief executives and other senior managers invest time in developing personal relationships.

To take the principle even further, allow potential suppliers to take you to lunch. These are the people, as we found earlier, that we are now being advised to "get over" ignoring when they send us emails soliciting our business. In the right circumstances, it can make sense not just to reply to the email but to meet them, particularly if lunch is on offer. There may be some useful competitive intelligence to be gleaned from the conversation and there is no telling what respective career paths you will both take in the future. There is little risk since all that is being invested is a little time.

Tackle the Difficult Issues

One of the benefits of being liberated from the cognition-draining impact of incessant emails and phone calls is the sensation of being clear-headed. This gives you a refreshing sense of perspective, but also allows you to anticipate the events that commonly knock us sideways. Almost any man-made disaster you can think of – and many natural ones, however dramatic and surprising - tends to follow a sustained period of warnings that went unheeded. This is true of 9/11, the global credit crunch, the Challenger space shuttle disaster and many others. Warnings are often ignored because most people who are in a position to do something about it are either too busy to notice or have an incentive not to disrupt the status quo.

The leader that has succeeded in putting the vicious circle of hyperactivity into reverse is well-placed to take note of warnings and anticipate difficulties. This may take the form of a difficult topic that colleagues duck rather than confront; it is called an "elephant in the room" since everyone can see it's there but no one wants to be the first to point it out. Just as it is crucial not to allow internal discord to fester, so it is necessary to confront issues that people prefer to leave unsaid. These may revolve around personalities or historical situations. My belief is that allowing such issues to continue will always rebound at some point, so it is better to bring everything out into the open.

A startling example of this failure to confront an open sore – in this case, in relationship terms – is offered by James Stewart's history of Disney. Michael Eisner's relationship with promising young hireling Jeffrey Katzenburg was disastrous almost from the outset. Under the heading for 'Katzenburg' in his book's index, Stewart lists 24 entries for the sub-heading: "Eisner's conflicts with." One such entry refers to one of many private dinners attended by the two men in failed attempts to restore the relationship. Their failure to confront issues was, on one occasion, described by Katzenburg as follows: "It was as though an elephant were sitting in a third chair at the table and neither [Eisner nor Katzenburg] said anything about it. Privately, Eisner was confiding to another book collaborator: "I think I hate the little midget." Disney ultimately fired Katzenburg – despite his huge commercial contribution – in a manner that was handled so poorly by Eisner that Katzenburg ultimately sued for $280m. He also started Dreamworks with Stephen Spielberg, giving Disney a formidable competitor in the animated feature market.

A further aspect of being clear-headed is that you will no longer crowd out those small thoughts and nagging doubts that have previously vied for attention with limitless messages and inconsequential activities. Listen to the small voices in the back of your mind, the fleeting questions and the uncomfortable impressions. These often turn out to have some sort of basis in fact and you will benefit from tackling issues head-on.

The Personal Dimension

There is much to dislike about the current vogue of CEO hyperactivity and its impact on families. However, the remark that I find most disturbing can be found, attributed to Jon Moulton of Alchemy Partners, in Tappin and Cave's *The Secrets of CEOs*. He explains why he prefers to invest in companies where the chief executive has been divorced:

"I take a lot of interest in the chief executive's marital status. One divorce is slightly better than none, because managers are motivated and challenged and sometimes they need to rebuild their wealth."

Writing as a one-time divorcé, I find this slightly disturbing as the sentiment is a short step away from attaching higher status to a divorced manager. Demands on chief executives are such that it is entirely normal to spend the working week in a city centre flat, returning to the large family home at weekends. Globalisation has resulted in international travel forming an ever larger part of the senior manager's working life. These situations put pressure on domestic life and stable marriages, as being away from home inevitably exposes the manager to situations that could erode a marital relationship. It is no different from the vet who has jars of ketamine staring at him from the shelves.

It is a pity that these modes of behaviour are often held as symbols of high status. It need not be the case that having a senior corporate job will lead to divorce (indeed only a small number of the CEOs interviewed by Cave and Tappin have been divorced), but it is easy to see a trend in which increasing hyperactivity correlates with a decline in virtues.

I have already observed that I find it interesting that Luke Johnson, a serial entrepreneur rather than moral philosopher, should describe the practice of using a BlackBerry in meetings as 'uncivil'. As we have seen in research such as the Good Samaritan experiment, there is a state of mind induced by external time pressure that erodes decency. A hyperactive working environment has a similar impact whereby messages are unacknowledged and people look at BlackBerrys while colleagues address meetings, even though research suggests that they know this to be wrong. The same lack of civility extends into our personal relationships. A July 2009 poll in *Glamour Magazine* suggests that most couples will have rows within two days of going on holiday and that the number one complaint for women is their partner looking at their BlackBerry (for the sake of completeness, men get annoyed about their partners over-packing).

Time Away from Work

Once you establish boundaries around use of email communications as outlined in Chapter Five, it becomes simpler to protect time with the family at home and on holiday. The detachment from work will deepen the sense of perspective and increase resilience when back at work.

Limiting Your Working Week

How many hours you work each week will depend to some extent on your overall relationship with work. If you subscribe to the distorted twenty-first century work ethic in which working excessive hours is an indicator of status, then you will experience consequences for your well-being and quality of life which will also impact your family and the people who work for you. Inverting the hyperactive mind-set can, however, bring numerous benefits. If you adopt the philosophy that working excessive hours indicates a failure to delegate, then your approach to people leadership will change.

The first step to changing your mind-set is the recognition that our capacity for high-performance work is not unlimited. I have reflected already that my personal upper limit was about 50 hours a week, beyond which each incremental hour at work became increasingly less effective. While people will vary in finding their natural threshold, this appears to be backed up by current research.

In the October 2009 issue of the *Harvard Business Review*, Leslie Perlow and Jessica Porter report that their research in 2008 showed that 94 per cent of 1000 people surveyed that were working in professional services (i.e. consultants, investment banker, lawyers, accountants etc.) worked more than 50 hours a week, with nearly half working more than 65 hours[li]. Additionally, they spent 20 to 25 hours each week on their BlackBerrys while outside the office. They followed this up with an experiment at strategy consultants Boston Consulting Group in which some case teams consultants were forced to take, in rotation, one day and one evening a week out of the office without checking voicemail or email. While there was, unsurprisingly, a good deal of resistance to this, the experiment was carried out and, after five months, research into the attitudes of consultants in both experiment teams and control teams showed the former scoring significantly higher across a number of dimensions; they reported higher job satisfaction, better work–life balance, greater learning development and significantly higher levels of open communication within their teams. In a finding that nullified early fears that clients would receive a reduced level of service, the research showed that the experiment teams reported higher levels of value delivery. As Perlow and Porter put it:

"When people are "always on", responsiveness becomes ingrained in the way they work, expected by clients and partners, and even institutionalised in performance metrics. There is no impetus to explore whether the work actually requires 24/7 responsiveness; to the contrary, people just work harder and longer, without considering how they could work better. Yet, what we discovered is that the cycle of 24/7 responsiveness can be broken if people collectively challenge the mind–set. Furthermore, new ways of working can be found that benefit not just individuals but the organization which gains in quality and efficiency – and, in the long run, experiences higher retention of more of its best people."

So the justification that clients require 24/7 responsiveness is often a myth. Both customer and supplier have been sucked into the vicious cycle of hyperactivity in which contact and messaging start to fuel their own momentum. Perlow and Porter's research shows that if you reverse the vicious cycle, the client's experience actually improves.

Holiday

If you are a salaried employee, even a very senior one, your contract with your employer includes a period of paid holiday. This could be as much as six weeks each year during which you are paid to get out of the office and enjoy yourself. *Take all your holiday.*

Holidays are an important event not just for personal relaxation and spending time with the family. From a professional point of view, the rest will make you more effective as a manager and leader. Furthermore, being away from the office even for a short period will give you a sense of perspective. By relaxing and removing yourself from the day-to-day bustle of the office, you will see things more clearly.

I used to work with a colleague who had developed the highly effective habit of booking her next holiday on the day she returned from her last one. This is actually a really smart thing to do since holidays are beneficial not just as they are experienced but as something to look forward to. If you know you are going away in say, six weeks, you can sustain a consistent work-rate in the knowledge that you have a break coming up.

Working too hard can become a vicious cycle in which you find yourself too busy and exhausted to organise a holiday. Without light at the end of the tunnel, work becomes an interminable drudge and the sense of exhaustion will deepen. When you do finally take a holiday, the likelihood is that your body will relax and succumb to illness within the first few days.

If email has become so prevalent in your organisation that people are deterred from taking holiday by the volume of emails expected on their return, then there is a serious problem.

In a 2006 *New York Times* article titled "The Rise of Shrinking-Vacation Syndrome", Timothy Egan wrote:

The Conference Board, a private research group, found that at the start of the summer, 40 percent of consumers had no plans to take a vacation over the next six months — the lowest percentage recorded by the group in 28 years. A survey by the Gallup Organization in May based on telephone interviews with a national sample of 1,003 adults found that 43 percent of respondents had no summer vacation plans.[lii]

While there are a range of factors contributing to this, the impact of technology-enabled communication is undoubtedly one of them. Egan goes on to cite the example of PriceWaterhouseCoopers recognising the problem and actually shutting down the office to stop people working, albeit for only ten days over Christmas and for five days around the Fourth of July. A partner in the company's human resources office is quoted as saying:

"We aren't doing this to push people out the door. But we wanted to create an environment where people could walk away and not worry about missing a meeting, a conference call or 300 e-mails."

If, like Michael Eisner, you would revel in being able to tell people that you had taken only one week as holiday in twenty-eight years, then this advice is not pertinent to you. Eisner has certainly achieved extraordinary personal wealth over the course of his career, although I would argue a punishing work schedule is not necessarily a condition of that level of success as I know others that have achieved comparable wealth *and* taken a full of quota family holidays. While there are inevitably other factors at play, I would be surprised if there were not some relationship between Eisner's work-rate at Disney and his need for emergency open-heart surgery.

Health, Fitness and Resilience

One of the most dramatically detrimental aspects of the 24/7 working lifestyle is the impact on health, both directly and indirectly. Psychologists and physiologists dispute the direct causal relationship between stress and illness; nevertheless, there are plenty of indirect drivers of poor health. Stress and a frenetic working life drive up consumption of alcohol, cigarettes, poor-quality foods and caffeine beyond the moderate levels at which they are harmless. This combines with – and in turn exacerbates – other drivers of ill-health such as weight gain, sleep deprivation, high blood pressure and high cholesterol. Many of these health issues are inextricably linked and fuel a vicious circle in which falling resilience through poor health leads to reduced effectiveness at work, hence more stress and still longer working hours.

We all have anecdotal experience of comparatively young managers falling seriously ill through poor lifestyle in which work was a factor. Doctors in emergency wards can tell of countless examples of powerful executives rushed in by ambulance having collapsed with a life-threatening illness. For a startling illustration of the impact of a range of health conditions on longevity, see the *British Medical Journal*'s June 2009 publication on life expectancy among civil servants. The publication was the conclusion of a piece of research that followed a cohort of 19,000 men over a period of 38 years. The research concluded that the 5 per cent of men with the poorest risk profiles (based on a number of factors that included smoking, cholesterol concentration, Body Mass Index and blood pressure) had a life expectancy beyond the age of 50 of *15 years less* than the men in top 5 per cent. The report breaks down each factor and calculates its impact on longevity; blood pressure alone accounts for a six-year range in life expectancy beyond 50.[liii] So if pressures of work are driving you to live an unhealthy lifestyle, it may ultimately result in you spending fewer years with your grandchildren after you retire.

If the vicious circle is reversed, a healthy lifestyle will make the leader more resilient and better equipped to deal with the demands of business and personal life.

Many successful leaders already manage to achieve parallel success in a sporting context. The booming triathlon industry comprises huge volumes of committed athletes that have adhered to grueling training schedules in order to prevail in such a demanding activity. Many of these are successful in business, and my anecdotal experience is that they tend to have also mastered balancing work and life.

There are several inter-related dimensions to becoming a healthy and resilient leader.

Exercise

It is not necessary to be a triathlete in order to become

sufficiently fit for successful leadership but a level of personal fitness will support greater resilience at work, happiness in both work and home life and will ultimately contribute to longevity.

Becoming fit inevitably involves a level of time-commitment, but reversing the vicious cycle of hyperactive work practices will free up abundant quantities of time in order to exercise.

Why exercise? For one thing, it will make you feel good. Exercise carried out over a sustained session releases endorphins; this is why returning from a run of five miles or so will make you feel uplifted and, paradoxically, give you energy. I am a great believer in running and personally aim to do three five-mile runs a week. I do this first thing in the morning. In addition to the physical health benefits, the solitude gives your brain some uninterrupted waking time in which to turn things over.

In addition to solitary exercise, it is helpful to take part in group activity since, as we shall see, social activity geographically close to your home can contribute to happiness. This might be a group of you that take a cycling trip once a week or, as I do, play doubles at tennis each week as part of a regular group of eight friends.

Competitive sports give an outlet for some of the reserves of energy you will discover when you become physically fit in a sustained way.

Diet

Hyperactive corporate life does not support a healthy diet and contributes to the growing blight of obesity and its consequent problems. A lifestyle of early mornings, late evenings, snatched meals and snacks along with punishing travel schedules all contribute to poor diet.

If weight is an issue, exercise is half of the equation in addressing this since this determines how much energy you burn off. The other half is what you take on. My own approach, as one prone to putting on weight, is to avoid all sweets, biscuits and snacks. I particularly steer clear of processed carbohydrates as medical advice suggests that these are readily turned to fat by our bodies – more so than fat itself. I eat a good breakfast of fruit followed by home-made birchen muesli; oats are slow-burn carbohydrates that contain a natural appetite suppressant. I try and eat a good cooked lunch with steamed vegetables and eat very lightly in the evening, often having simply a smoothie with fruit, nuts, yoghurt – and more oats. My experience is that there is truth in the old adage of breakfasting like a king but dining in the evening like a pauper.

If a good diet is combined with regular exercise, it is still possible to lose weight and still have the occasional blow-out; this might be a meal out socially or an important business dinner with clients.

"Hydration" – or drinking water – is, to my mind,

over-played. Remarkably, organisations have begun to intervene in this area. Lucy Kellaway wrote in the *Financial Times* in November 2009 of a large corporate placing a bottle of water on the desk of every employee in an eleven-storey building. Beside each bottle was placed:

"a little card displaying a series of yellow blobs from the palest lemon to the deepest ochre. This represented the colour of urine depending on how much water had been consumed and was meant to tell employees whether they ought to be drinking more. Dehydrated workers were less productive, the card warned."[liv]

This nannyish approach to water consumption can have disastrous consequences. In 2001, "nutritional therapist" Barbara Nash put a client on her "Amazing Hydration Diet" which involved increasing water intake hugely while cutting out salt in her diet. The resulting uncontrollable vomiting was explained as "part of the detoxification process" and she was told to increase water intake still further by six pints a day; the client ended up in intensive care with life-threatening sodium deficiency and endured permanent brain damage.

This is another of those aspects of modern life that can be enriched by an understanding of our ancestral environment where water was a scarce resource. Over millions of years, our ancestors responded to the natural impulse of thirst and sought out water. So, drink when you are thirsty. There is probably no need to carry a five-litre plastic container of water with you wherever you go as I have seen one businesswoman do. There is probably also no need to clutch a special plastic water-bottle complete with hand-grip when you are out for a jog. Our ancestors ran miles and miles after prey without bottles of water. Read T.E.Lawrence's *Seven Pillars of Wisdom* on how Arab tribesmen survived during desert campaigns on minute quantities of water.

In large quantities, tea, coffee and alcohol are bad for your diet. In moderation, I believe they are fine. The diuretic and dehydration impacts of tea and coffee are disputed. Research conducted by scientists at the Center for Human Nutrition in Omaha and published in the *Journal of the American College of Nutrition* found "no significant differences at all"[lv] in hydration levels of those drinking tea, coffee and caffeinated drinks and those abstaining. More than one alcoholic drink, however, will affect hydration. Drinking coffee will not dehydrate you but it may inhibit sleep if consumed late in the day as it has a half-life of six to nine hours.

Sleep

Good quality sleep is under threat from the 24/7 work ethic, the ubiquity of information technology – most obviously in the form of the BlackBerry under the pillow, and the other detractors of good health such as stress, obesity and excessive intake of alcohol and caffeine. We have seen the impact of the corrupted Protestant work ethic and shown, in the dramatic personal example of Frank Wells of Disney, that it is possible to approach sleep as an undesirable human failing that stands between you and working yet more hours. Wells was known to fall asleep in meetings and was lauded for this at his funeral by Disney's CEO Michael Eisner who described sleep as Wells's "enemy."

I take a different view on the subject of sleep and would make the interview with Harvard Medical School Professor Dr Charles Czeisler in the October 2006 edition of the *Harvard Business Review* required reading for all leaders. Czeisler is Harvard Medical School's Baldino Professor of Sleep Medicine and knows a thing or two about the impact of too little sleep.

The impact of sleep deprivation on cognitive performance is well-established. Just as interruptions can inhibit performance, going without sleep for 18 consecutive hours will be detrimental to reaction speed, both short- and long-term memory, ability to focus, decision-making capacity, cognitive speed and spatial orientation. If we limit our nightly sleep allowance to less than six hours for several consecutive nights, then a sleep deficit will multiply these factors.

We need good quality sleep in order to function properly and, as we get older, it becomes naturally harder to achieve. Once we are past the age of 40, our sleep becomes more fragmented as we are more sensitive to noise, our own increasing bodily aches and pains and the onset of sleep disorders such as apnea, when breathing briefly ceases causing us to wake up.

Sleep is intrinsically linked to other elements of a healthy lifestyle, particularly diet. Putting on too much weight, eating late into the evening and taking in caffeine late in the day all impinge on quality of sleep. The relationship works in reverse, too; chronic sleep restriction increases levels of appetite and reduces your ability to metabolise glucose – this increases the body's production of the hormone ghrelin which in turn makes you crave carbohydrates and sugars.

Czeisler equates the machismo "always-on" culture that equates sleeplessness with high performance as akin to the bygone era in which men that could "hold their drink" were celebrated:

"It amazes me that contemporary work and social culture glorifies sleeplessness in the way we once glorified people who could hold their liquor. We now know that 24 hours without sleep or a week of sleeping four or five hours a night induces an impairment equivalent to a blood alcohol level of 0.1%. We would never say, 'This person is a great worker! He's drunk all the time!' yet we continue to celebrate people who sacrifice sleep."[lvi]

The comparison with alcohol is a pertinent one since sleep-deprived drivers cause road accidents even though lack of sleep is not stigmatised in the same way as driving under the influence of alcohol. In the US, drowsy drivers are responsible for 20 per cent of road accidents and some 8000 deaths a year; there are numerous cases of drivers killing innocent motorists or pedestrians after going without sufficient sleep for a sustained period.

The idea of taking a nap in the afternoon would be regarded as completely heretical in most organisations but the concept of the "siesta" has a long tradition in Mediterranean Europe. In 2007 France's Health Minister was ridiculed for sponsoring a revival of "la sieste" – however, short "power-naps" help with the effects of sleep deprivation described by Dr Czeisler. In the October 2009 issue of the *Harvard Business Review*, psychiatry professor Robert Stickgold extols the virtues of taking a few minutes of shut-eye. There is evidence of an improvement in performance, and he cites a New Zealand study of air-traffic controllers that scored better on alertness tests if they took a planned nap of 40 minutes during their shift.[lvii]

A report in the June 2009 *Proceedings of the National Academy of Science* shows that a nap with REM (Rapid Eye

Movement) sleep improves problem-solving and boosts memory. Is this beginning to be reflected in working life? Google has introduced nap pods that allow employees to block out sound and light; I have met a highly successful entrepreneur who has a similar pod in his office.

Sleep is an under-acknowledged contributor to health and well-being and needs to be recognised as such both for you personally as a leader and for the people that work for you.

The Hinterland

I believe it is also important for the corporate person to have a hinterland, a world away from work. Sometimes, this means actively making time to pursue a sport or activity and keeping to it. It also refers to the rich world of art, be it visiting an art exhibition, listening to music or reading a novel. I am dismayed when I meet an educated business leader who admits (sometimes as if it's a badge of honour) that they have not had time to read a novel for years.

If Harold Macmillan could find time to work through the great Victorian novelists while he was Prime Minister, then contemporary leaders should be able to do likewise. I favour Anthony Trollope whose sweeping Barchester Chronicles – over six large novels – give a sense of perspective that provides a welcome antidote to the rushed pace of twenty-first century life. Trollope was remarkable not just as a prolific novelist but also for his achievements as a senior civil servant in the Post Office.

Developing a hinterland can also be a vehicle for utilising your skills and experience in a way that helps your community. This might mean serving on the board of a charity that raises money for a cause close to your heart; there are reasons for doing this beyond simple altruism – my experience is that this can yield insights and contacts that enrich your mainstream professional life.

Happiness

Social scientists are beginning to get a firm grasp around the science of happiness and what contributes to it. The human animal is not, of course, "designed" to be happy – its purpose, as with other living creatures, is to perpetuate its genetic inheritance. However, certain themes endure in the best studies of personal happiness:

Family: The fact that one's immediate family is a source of personal happiness should be a truism. But when one considers how frequently work erodes our family relationships, it is worth restating its importance. A hyperactive approach to work encroaches hugely on one's family; your spouse endures sustained periods of absence from the home and reduced attentiveness on those occasions when you are home. This might manifest itself in the form of continuous BlackBerry use, tiredness or irritability. In extreme circumstance, high levels of travel and sustained contact with colleagues provide an environment for extra-marital relationships that could fracture the family unit. Children may miss out on quality contact with parents and could grow up to describe themselves as "BlackBerry Orphans".

Friends: A close circle of peers – preferably outside the immediate work environment – with whom one can relax is another important driver of happiness. This might take the form of a golf tour, a diving trip or a regular tennis game. These are friends with whom it should be possible to chat openly about work pressures without the concern that it will get back to somebody in the office. These sorts of activity can readily be missed or fail to happen due to the difficulty of aligning diaries or the lack of will to organise it. It is worth making the effort to set aside time for these sorts of pursuits.

Community: Having a strong connection with people who live in your immediate geographic vicinity has been identified as a strong driver of happiness. This makes sense when one considers the communal nature of our lives in the ancestral environment. While many small villages have a strong sense of community and a packed calendar of social events, the experience for many leaders and managers living in metropolitan areas is often different. While they may have a strong network of friends and family, they may be isolated in their immediate locale. It is not uncommon for families in suburban houses to live next door to a family for 20 years and never exchange a word with them. As with other aspects of twenty-first century life, we accept this as the norm and become inured to it to some extent.

I recently met someone who bought an expensive house in the Home Counties on a prestigious estate surrounded by other highly successful executives and their families. He moved within a year as he never met any of his neighbours, who all lived in splendid isolation behind high walls and security gates. Each neighbour – when in residence and not abroad with their work – would leave the house to go to work in the very early hours and not return until late at night.

Living in an area where there is some sense of community and having a positive connection with immediate neighbours has a surprisingly positive uplift on happiness. As well as casual neighbourly contact, social activity might revolve around a sports or leisure club, religious place of worship or school. Moving house comes with a large price tag and so it is worth considering these factors when choosing where to live.

Sense of purpose: We need activity. Boredom can drive stress, possibly to the same extent as overwork. For most of us, our sense of purpose derives from our career and therefore our choice of career is an important determinant of our happiness. Many leaders and managers work hard without any strong personal attachment to their jobs, companies or industries. Not everybody can find vocations about which they are passionate, but it is easy to become accustomed over a working lifetime to doing a job that you do not particularly like.

Wealth: Money is, let's face it, important. But pursuing the attainment of wealth as an exclusive route to happiness can be a mistake. This is because while people think they are pursuing wealth, they rarely have an absolute achievement in mind; what they are more frequently pursuing is status and, in relative terms, they will always find themselves confronted by somebody with more wealth and, hence, more status. I was once at a lavish corporate sporting event as a guest of one of the UK's top 100 companies. The CEO shuffled up to one of the other guests who, having spent an hour so queuing to get into the car park, was staring wistfully at the stream of helicopters dropping guests off at the far end of the site. "Ah," said the CEO with a sense of recognition in his voice. "You've got helicopter envy." I was also told of a successful British entrepreneur who sold his company and bought an ostentatiously large yacht. He sailed it to Puerto Banus in Spain and was happily in the process of docking it, champagne flute in hand, when he was cast into darkness by the shadow of a far larger yacht pulling in alongside him.

I have met a number of very wealthy people and they seem to me to have about the same mix of happiness and sadness as the rest of the population. Their happiness seems to me to be determined not by their wealth but by a combination of all the factors listed above along with the extent to which they are satisfied with their success on an objective level.

My favourite anecdote comes from Lucy Kellaway's column in the *Financial Times*. She tells of a friend invited on to the enormous boat of a multi-millionaire who complained that he was no longer able to afford his own private jet and, because of straitened circumstances, was forced to share. When someone observed that Roman Abramovitch had two such jets, the tycoon's wife was heard to mutter: "How the other half live."

Endnote

Just like addiction, hyperactivity at work is a choice. This fact should be reassuring since it suggests that we have the capacity to change it. There is a limit to what we can do about our environment when we are part of a large organisation unless we are in a position of leadership. Yet, the more senior we are, the more impact we are able to have and, since leaders have an increasing impact on the quality of life of the people that work for them, I suggest there is a duty of care on employers that looks to the quality of the working life of their employees and the extent to which work bleeds into their family life. For the organisation, there is a rationale of self-interest in limiting ineffective activity, because this will ultimately improve employee satisfaction, reduce churn and increase productivity.

If the research conducted by Nathan Zeldes on the impacts of the inefficient use of email and digital interruptions were only half true for any organisation in question, this would still amount to some 10 per cent of payroll costs being spent unproductively. If anything external to the company had half of that impact – say, a toxic dump next to its headquarters causing absentee levels of five per cent – then the leadership of that organisation would surely act very decisively on the issue. Hyperactivity is harder to fix since, unlike so many occupational challenges from the past, it is often worst among an organisation's leadership; they are often complicit in the behaviours that have allowed it to become endemic.

There is clearly a moral dimension to this. We have seen that research such as the Darley and Batson "Good Samaritan" study has demonstrated that in a context of hustle and time pressure, we unconsciously lower the threshold of what we consider to be a minimum level of acceptable behaviour. This is evidenced by a lack of courtesy in the way we ignore others' messages or look at our mobile devices when in meetings with colleagues. Worse still, this affects our relationships with friends and families.

Continued advances in communications technology will only exacerbate the problem. As the number of channels continues to multiply, our frequency of contact will carry on climbing. What we need to understand is that contact does not constitute communication and, to paraphrase T.S.Eliot, information does not constitute knowledge. Where I would argue that the knowledge gap is greatest of all is in the area of self-knowledge: the aspects of human psychology that drive us to work in the way that we do. Evolutionary theory offers an illuminating lens through which to view the twenty-first century workplace and I have shown how the centrality of status to our lives and our thirst for gossip – both formed in our ancestral environment – have collided with the mobile and multi-channel attributes of modern communications in what we might call a "perfect storm" of hyperactivity.

Much is said and written about "work-life balance". This concept is outmoded since work and life outside work are no longer polar opposites in an equation, which suggests taking from one will have an impact on the other. In the first instance, many are not in control of the volume of work that they have to confront and are not in a position to do anything about it impinging on "life". For those who are in control, many often lack the will to reduce the impact of work on the rest of their lives. They are seduced by the cult of hyperactivity which lends a sense of importance to their lives and cultivates the impression of high status even if, at home, they are reading emails when they should be reading bed-time stories to their children.

What I hope this book has offered is a vision of work in which the concept of the virtuous leader is more attractive than a frenetic, hyperactive one. Virtuous in this context means celebrating a life outside work because it makes one more effective in work; it means success and enjoyment in both work and personal lives being inter-related and self-fuelling. It means not taking the burdens of leadership entirely on your own shoulders but learning to delegate and leverage the organisation. Ultimately, it is about the difference between being known as the most prolific emailer around or being able to remember your kids growing up.

APPENDIX – DAN LOEB EMAIL

From: U.K. Jobseeker
Sent: Tuesday, March 22, 2005 11:34 AM
To: Daniel Loeb

Subject: CV

Daniel,
Thanks for calling earlier today. Enclosed is my CV for your review. I look forward to following up with you when you have more time.
Best regards,
U.K. Jobseeker

————————————————

————-Original Message————-
From: Daniel Loeb
To: U.K. Jobseeker
Subject: RE: CV

What are your 3 best current European ideas?
Daniel S. Loeb

Managing Member
Third Point LLC
360 Madison Avenue, 24th floor
New York, NY 10017
212 224 7400

From: U.K. Jobseeker
To: Daniel Loeb
Subject: RE: CV

Daniel,

I am sorry but it does not interest me to move forward in this way. If you wish to have a proper discussion about what you are looking to accomplish in Europe, and see how I might fit in, fine.

Lesson one of dealing in Europe, business is not conducted in the same informal manner as in the U.S.

Best regards,

U.K. Jobseeker

————-Original Message————-
From: Daniel Loeb
To: U.K. Jobseeker
Subject: RE: CV

One idea would suffice.

We are an aggressive performance oriented fund looking for blood thirsty competitive individuals who show initiative and drive to make outstanding investments. This is why I have built Third Point into a $3.0 billion fund with average net returns of 30% net over 10 years.

We find most brits are bit set in their ways and prefer to knock back a pint at the pub and go shooting on weekend rather than work hard.

Lifestyle choices are important and knowing one's limitations with respect to dealing in a competitive environment is too. That is Lesson 1 at my shop.

It is good that we learned about this incompatibility early in the process and I wish you all the best in your career in traditional fund management.

Daniel Loeb

CEO

From: U.K. Jobseeker
To: Daniel Loeb
Subject: RE: CV

Daniel,

I guess your reputation is proven correct. [...] I did not achieve the success I have by knocking back a pint, as you say. I am aggressive, and I do love this business. I [... have] spent more than half my life on this side of the pond I think I know a little something about how one conducts business in the UK and Europe.

There are many opportunities in the UK and Europe, shareholder regard is only beginning to be accepted and understood. However, if you come here and handle it in the same brash way you have in the U.S. I guarantee you will fail. Things are done differently here, yes place in society still matters, where one went to school etc. It will take tact, and patience (traits you obviously do not have) to succeed in this arena.

Good luck!

U.K. Jobseeker

——-Original Message——-
From: Daniel Loeb
To: U.K. Jobseeker
Cc: [board member at German asset manager]
Subject: RE: CV

Well, you will have plenty of time to discuss your "place in society" with the other fellows at the club.

I love the idea of a [...] unemployed guy [...] telling me that I am going to fail.

At Third Point, like the financial markets in general, "one's place in society" does not matter at all. We are a bunch of scrappy guys from diverse backgrounds (Jewish Muslim, Hindu etc) who enjoy outwitting pompous asses like yourself in financial markets globally.

Your "inexplicable insouciance" and disrespect is fascinating; it must be a French/English aristocratic thing. I will be following your "career" with great interest.

I have copied [board member at German asset manager] so that he can introduce you to people who might be a better fit—there must be an insurance company or mutual fund out there for you.

Dan Loeb

From: U.K. Jobseeker
To: Daniel Loeb
Subject: RE: CV

Hubris

From: Daniel Loeb
To: U.K. Jobseeker
Subject: RE: CV
Laziness

REFERENCES

[i] Peter Hennessy (2006). *Having it so Good. Britain in the Fifties.* Allen Lane

[ii] Iain Martin. "Indiscipline, chaos and decay: this is how governments die." *Daily Telegraph.* London. 27 February 2009

[iii] Steve Tappin and Andrew Cave (2008). *The Secrets of CEOs.* Nicholas Brealey

[iv] Economic & Social Research Council (2001). "Willing Slaves: Employment in Britain in the 21st Century".

[v] "Work Your Proper Hours Day: The Manager's Guide". TUC. (2006)

[vi] British Social Attitudes Report. "Perspectives on a Changing Society." 24 January 2007

[vii] Stephen Barley & Deborah Knight (1992). "Toward a cultural theory of stress complaints". *Research in Organizational Behaviour.* 14, 1-48

[viii] Samaritans "Stressed Out" Survey (2006)

[ix] Katherine Rosman. "BlackBerry Orphans." *Wall Street Journal.* New York. 8 December 2006

[x] "Exec: Email is causing killer stress." *Independent.* London. 25 September 2009

[xi] Nathan Zeldes, David Sward & Sigal Louchheim (2007) "Infomania: Why we can't afford to ignore it any longer" *First Monday:* 12 (8)

[xii] Thomas Jackson, Ray Dawson & Darren Wilson. "Case Study: Evaluating the Effect of Email Interruptions within the Workplace" Working paper

[xiii] AOL Email Addiction Survey, July 2008

[xiv] Christina Cavanagh (2004). "Email in the Workplace: Coping with Overload" Working paper

[xv] Pitney Bowes (1998). "Pitney Bowes study finds messaging creates greater stress at work"

xvi O'Conaill, B., & Frohlich, D. (1995). Timespace in the workplace: Dealing with interruptions. *Proceedings of Computer-Human Interaction '95,* Denver, Colorado, New York: ACM Press, 262–263

xvii Glenn Wilson (2005). "Infomania" study. www.drglennwilson.com

xviii Microsoft Office Personal Productivity Challenge (2005)

xix Adam Bryant. "Feeling All Thumbed Out." *New York Times.* New York. 28 May 2006

xx Andrew Cave. Aidan Heavey Profile. *Sunday Telegraph.* London. 29 August 2009

xxi Emma Cook. "The Rules for Balancing Technology and Relationships." *The Times.* London. 13 June 2009

xxii Jeffrey A.Schaler (2000). "*Addiction is a Choice.*" Open Court.

xxiii Suw Charman-Anderson. "Breaking the Email Compulsion." *Guardian.* London. 28 August 2008

xxiv APS Survey of email stress (2003). Melbourne, Australian Psychological Society

xxv Nicholson, N. (2000). *Managing the Human Animal.* Crown Publishers, New York

xxvi Wright, R. (1994). *The Moral Animal. Evolutionary Psychology and Everyday Life.* Pantheon Books

xxvii Emler, N. (2009). Speaker notes from talk "Why Humans Gossip". British Science Festival; 7 September 2009

xxviii Poldrack, R. (2009). *Multi-tasking: The Brain Seeks Novelty. www.huffingtonpost.com* 28 October 2009

xxix Renaud, K., Ramsay, J., Hair, M. (2009). "You've Got E-Mail!"… Shall I Deal With It Now? Electronic Mail From the Recipient's Perspective. *International Journal of Human-Computer Interaction.* 21(3), 313–332

xxx Hobson, D. (1990). *The Pride of Lucifer. The Unauthorised Biography of Morgan Grenfell.* Hamish Hamilton, London.

xxxi Lewis, M. (1989) *Liar's Poker.* Hodder and Stoughton, London

xxxii *Financial Times,* 1 April 2005

xxxiii Jackall, R. (1988). *Moral Mazes. The World of Corporate Managers.* Oxford University Press

xxxiv Meyer, C. (2005). *DC Confidential.* Weidenfeld & Nicolson, London.

[xxxv] Stewart, J.B. (2005). *DisneyWar. The Battle for the Magic Kingdom.* Simon & Schuster

[xxxvi] Source: email; author unknown

[xxxvii] Leo Babauta, zenhabits.net

[xxxviii] Cavanagh, C.A. (2004). Email in the Workplace: Coping with Overload.

[xxxix] Schipley, D. & Schwalbe, W. (2007). *Send. The How, Why, When and When Not of Email.* Alfred A. Knopf

[xl] Koch, R. (1997). *The 80/20 Principle. The Secret of Achieving More with Less.* Nicholas Brealey

[xli] Just, M.A. et al (2001). Interdependence of Nonoverlapping Cortical Systems in Dual Cognitive Tasks. *NeuroImage* 14, 417–426

[xlii] Gladwell, M. (2000). *The Tipping Point. How Little Things can Make a Big Difference.* Little, Brown & Co.

[xliii] Darley, J.M. & Batson, C.D. (1973) "From Jerusalem to Jericho: A study of situational and dispositional variables in helping behaviors". *Journal of Personality and Social Psychology* 27; 1, 100-108

[xliv] Johnson, L. *Financial Times.* 24 June 2009

[xlv] Kirsner, S. (2008) boston.com, 2 November 2008

[xlvi] Collins, J.C. & Porras, J.I. (1994). *Built to Last: Successful Habits of Visionary Companies.* HarperBusiness

[xlvii] Diamond, J. (1992). *The Third Chimpanzee. The Evolution and Future of the Human Animal.* HarperCollins.

[xlviii] Rich Harris, J. (1998). *The Nurture Assumption. Why Children Turn Out the Way They Do.* Bloomsbury

[xlix] Tajfel, H. (1970). Experiments in Intergroup Discrimination. *Scientific American*, 223, 96-102

[l] Scandura, T. (1998). Dysfunctional Mentoring Relationships and Outcomes. *Journal of Management.* 24 (3); 449-467

[li] Perlow, L.A. & Porter, J.L. (2009). Making Time Off Predictable and Required. *Harvard Business Review;* October 2009

[lii] Egan, T. (2006). *New York Times*

[liii] Clarke, R. et al (2009). Life expectancy in relation to cardiovascular risk factors: 38 year follow-up of 19,000 men in the Whitehall study. *British Medical Journal.* 339:b3513

[liv] Kellaway, L. (2009). Financial Times

[lv] Grandjean, A.C. et al. (2000). The Effect of Caffeinated, Non-Caffeinated, Caloric and Non-Caloric Beverages on Hydration. *Journal of the American College of Nutrition*. 19 (5); 591-600

[lvi] Czeisler, C.A. (2006). Sleep Deficit: The Performance Killer. *Harvard Business Review*. October 2006.

[lvii] Stickgold, R. (2009). The Simplest Way to Reboot your Brain. *Harvard Business Review*. October 2009.

Index

Addiction is a Choice, 42
Alchemy Partners, 170
Alex cartoons, 64
AOL, 31, 40
Australian Psychological Society, 48

Babauta, Leo, 71
Barley, Stephen, 15, 19
Batson, C. Daniel, 119, 194
Baylis, Dr Nick, 7
BBC, 25, 71
BlackBerry, 4, 18, 25,28, 37-54, 59, 70-71, 81-81, 91-97, 111, 113, 119, 122-3, 126, 167, 171-3, 184, 189
Boston Consulting Group, 173
British Medical Journal, 178
British Social Attitudes Report, 12, 17
Brown, Gordon, 2
Bryant, Adam, 38-9, 41
Built to Last, 126, 131, 133

Cannon, Walter B., 14
Carnegie Mellon University, 106
Cauldwell, John, 70
Cavanagh, Christina, 32, 86
Cave, Andrew, 3, 170-1
Center for Cognitive Brain Imaging, 106
Chase Manhattan Bank, 26
Churchill, Winston, 1-3, 9
Collins, Jerry, 126, 131, 133
Constant Contact, 124
Cooper, Professor Cary, 25
Czeiser, Dr Charles, 184-6

Daily Telegraph, 2
Darley, John M., 119, 194

Darnwood Group, 30
Darwin, Charles, 136
Deloites, 71
Descent of Man, The, 136
Diamond, Jared, 136
Disney, 65-6, 99, 132-3, 169-170, 177, 184
Dinsey War, 65
DreamWorks, 132, 170
Dunbar, Robin, 140-141
Dun's Review, 133

Economic and Social Research Council, 4, 10
Egan, Marsha, 44
Egan, Timothy, 176
Eighty-Twenty Principle, The, 98
Eisner, Michael, 65-6, 99-100, 132-3, 169-170, 177, 184
Email, 5, 14, 24-54, 59, 61, 66, 69, 70-94, 97, 102, 103, 106, 110, 111, 112, 113, 115, 116, 119, 122, 124-5, 135, 152-3, 165, 167, 168, 174, 176, 193, 195, 196
Emler, Nicholas, 50
Evolutionary theory, 49-51, 194

Financial Times, The, 182, 192
France Telecom, 25
Fundamental Attribution Error, 121

Gekko, Gordon, 60-1
Gladwell, Malcolm, 119-20, 139-141
Glamour Magazine, 172
Goodman, Gail, 124
Gore Associates, 139-141
Gutfreund, John, 61

Hair, Mario, 53
Harcourt, Lord, 55
Harvard Business Review, 173, 184, 186
Heavey, Aidan, 39
Hewlett, Packard, 34
Hobson, Dominic, 55
Huffington Post, 52
Human Capital Accounting, 128

Inbox Zero, 90
Information Overload Research Group, 29
Intel, 29, 32, 35

Jackall, Robert, 62, 111
Jackson, Tom, 29-31, 33, 52
Johnson, Luke, 123, 171
Journal of Organizational Behaviour, 49
Journal of the American College of Nutrition, 183
Just, Marcel, 107

Kakabadse, Professor Nada, 40
Karoshi, 9, 80
Katzenberg, Jeffrey, 65, 132
Kellaway, Lucy, 182, 192
Kerviel, Jerome, 67
Kidulthood, 18
Kirsner, Scott, 124
Knight, Deborah, 15, 19
Koch, Richard, 98-9

Leighton, Allan, 150-1
Lewis, Michael, 63-4
Liar's Poker, 63-4
Loeb, Daniel, 61, 66, 197-201
Loughborough University, 30, 33

Macmillan, Harold, 3, 187
Managing the Human Animal, 49-51

Mann, Merlin, 90
Martin, Iain, 2
McKinsey Quarterly, 133
Meyer, Sir Christopher, 64-5
Microsoft, 23, 34, 36, 84, 85, 90, 91, 94
Microsoft Outlook, 34, 84-5, 89-91
Moral Animal, The, 49-57
Moral Mazes: The World of Corporate Managers, 62, 111
Moran, Lord, 1
Morgan Grenfell, 55
Moulton, John, 170

New York Times, 38, 176
Nicholson, Nigel, 49, 51, 167
Nielsen Media Research, 75
Northampton University, 40
Nurture Assumption, The, 137

OECD, 68-9

Pareto, Vilfredo, 99
Peattie, Charles, 64
Pellissier, Gervais, 26
Perlow, Leslie, 173-5
Pitney Bowes, 33
Poldrack, Russell, 52
Portas, Mike, 126, 131, 133
Porter, Jessica, 173-5
PriceWaterhouseCoopers, 176
Pride of Lucifer, The, 55
ProCare Health, 79
Procter & Gamble, 133
Pursuit of Happyness, The, 63

Ramsay, Judith, 53
Ranieri, Lewie, 63
Renaud, Karen, 53
Rich Harris, Judith, 137
Ross, Lee, 121
Royal Mail, 151

Saint Ignacius, 103
Salamon Brothers, 61
Samaritans, 13, 15, 19
Schaler, Jeffrey A., 42-4
Schjelderup-Ebbe, Thorlief, 58
Schwalbe, Will, 79
Secrets of CEOs, The, 3, 133, 170
Self Help, 62
Send, 79
Shipley, David, 79
Skandia, 129
Smiles, Samuel, 62
Social networking, 28, 72
Societe Generale, 67
Stafford, Tom, 43
Stewart, James B., 65, 99, 169
Stone, Oliver, 60
Stress, 4, 7, 12-24, 25-26, 34, 35,
46, 67, 74, 75, 77, 85, 106, 116, 178,
184, 190
Sunday Telegraph, 39

Tajfel, Henri, 137-8
Tappin, Steve, 3, 170-1
Taylor, Russell, 64
Third Chimpanzee, The, 136
Times, The, 40, 123
Tipping Point, The, 119, 139
Toyota, 9
TUC, 4, 10
Tullow Oil, 39
Twitter, 27, 72

University of Sheffield, 43

Walker, Vicki, 79
Wall Street (film), 60
Wall Street Journal, 18
Wells, Frank, 65, 184
Wilson, Glenn, 34, 91, 122
Wright, Robert, 49, 57-8

Zeldes, Nathan, 29, 32, 35-6, 106,
193

About the Author

Following a degree in English Literature at Magdalen College, Oxford, Ian began his career at strategy consultants LEK Consulting before spending almost two decades in management and leadership roles in the telecommunications and payments industries. While at BT, he conceived and launched BT Answer 1571 and was founding CEO of BT Click&Buy. He subsequently led two technology start-ups, latterly as CEO of AIM-listed Broca plc.

Following the acquisition of his last company, and having witnessed the impact of communications technology on the world of work, Ian embarked on a MSc in Organisational Behaviour at Birkbeck College, London where his research dissertation was an international study of the relationship between BlackBerry use and stress. He now writes, speaks and consults on leadership behaviours, work-life balance and how to get the best out of communications technology.

ian.price@grimsdykeconsulting.com
www.grimsdykeconsulting.com